Why People
Buy Things
They Don't
Need

Marketing Books from PMP

The Kids Market: Myths & Realities

Marketing to American Latinos, Part I

The Mirrored Window: Focus Groups from a Moderator's Point of View

The Great Tween Buying Machine

Marketing Insights to Help Your Business Grow

India Business

Marketing to American Latinos, Part II

Why People Buy Things They Don't Need

Pamela N. Danziger

PARAMOUNT MARKET PUBLISHING, INC.

39780

Paramount Market Publishing, Inc.
301 S. Geneva Street, Suite 109
Ithaca, NY 14850
www.paramountbooks.com
Telephone: 607-275-8100; 888-787-8100
Facsimile: 607-275-8101

Publisher: James Madden
Editorial Director: Doris Walsh

Book design: Peter Krakow
Cover design: Paperwork
All trademarks are the property of their respective companies.

Paramount Market Publishing's books are available at special discounts for bulk purchases for sales promotions or premiums. Special editions, including personalized covers, excerpts of existing books, and corporate imprints, can be created in large quantities for special needs. For more information, write to Special Markets, Paramount Market Publishing, 301 South Geneva Street, Suite 109, Ithaca, NY 14850, or e-mail: editors@paramountbooks.com

Library of Congress Catalog Number:
Cataloging in Publication Data available
ISBN 0-9671439-9-3

1 2 3 4 5 6 7 8 9 0

Table of Contents

INTRODUCTION

WHY PEOPLE BUY: THE KEY THAT UNLOCKS FUTURE MARKETING SUCCESS

In the marketing world, conventional wisdom holds that marketers do not need to know *why* consumers behave as they do. Ultimately all that really counts is who consumers are and how they behave: what they buy, where they buy it, when they buy it; and how much they spend. I don't dispute the critical importance of understanding the who, what, where, when, and how much of consumer behavior. It is the only gauge we have of marketing success.

However, by understanding *why* consumers behave as they do, you have a looking glass into the future. Understanding why helps a company anticipate and prepare for changes in the cultural, economic, and political environments. It provides insight into how predictable changes in consumer demographics will influence consumer behavior. Why consumers buy is the secret of predicting consumer behavior in a changing, shifting world.

TO ACCURATELY PREDICT THE FUTURE, YOU'VE GOT TO UNDERSTAND WHY

Every business executive wants to know—indeed, *demands* to know—the future. Yet, the research tools that are most frequently called upon to help anticipate the future are worthless to that end. We study the who, what, where, when, and how much, related to consumers. But this is the past, and it only tells us about the way the marketplace has been, not how it is going to be. Working under the erroneous assumption that the past is the best predictor of the future, we study, quantify, validate, and make predictions and projections on historical, but ultimately meaningless, data. Moreover, we feel comfortable and safe because all that studying, quantifying, validating, predicting, and projecting results in executive presentations and reports filled with neat charts, tables, and graphs. They give us confidence and take away our feelings of uncertainty and confusion. All our efforts and resources directed at predicting the future based upon the past are futile in the face of events like September 11, 2001.

9/11 MARKED A SHOCKING SHIFT IN CONSUMER PSYCHOLOGY

This likely would be a very different book had the terrible events of 9/11 not occurred. With research for this book started in May 2001 and concluded the first week in September 2001, I was busily analyzing data and writing my first draft on Tuesday morning, September 11th. After a couple of days of being glued to the television set, completely incapable of working and wondering whether work would ever matter again, my clear-eyed editor and friend of many years, Doris Walsh, helped me realize that with all that had happened, marketers would need to understand, maybe even more than ever before, why people buy things they don't need and whether they would be willing to continue buying in the face of such uncertainty. So in an effort toward personal healing and getting the book back on track, I returned to my manuscript and research notes and wrote a press release that was distributed over the Businesswire seven days after the attacks.

As president of Unity Marketing, the media call me regularly for information and commentary, but I have never gotten such a response from a single press release before. *USA Today*, *The Wall Street Journal*, *New York Times*, *Los Angeles Times*, and the *Early Today Show* all picked it up.

With the year 2001 holiday shopping season over, my predictions in that release proved correct. Consumers immediately and decisively turned away from luxury. After watching those Twin Towers fall, fears of using credit cards to shop over the internet were less threatening than being in a shopping mall with thousands of other people, and consumers started to shop online like never before. The holiday toy season was strictly back to basics with the 37-year-old GI Joe an unexpected best seller in the fad-driven world of toys. The 2001 holiday season was a bittersweet mix of pain and joy as we clung ever so tightly to those we love, in the warmth and security of our own homes.

How did I get it right? Not because I could foresee the terrible terrorist attacks, but because I knew and understood the "why" behind consumer behavior. My hypothesis˙ is that like one's personality, *the why that drives consumer behavior is remarkably stable throughout life.* By understanding the underlying why, we can predict how changes in the external environment will affect consumer behavior. In essence, whereas the who, what, where, when and how much of consumer behavior fluctuates, the *why* remains fixed and can be used to predict how change will impact the other aspects of consumer behavior. That was what enabled me to predict accurately how the post-9/11 holiday season would play out at the nation's cash registers.

The why remains fixed and can be used to predict consumer behavior.

With our country at war, we have all learned the critical importance of "human intelligence" in the political and military arenas. In fact, many analysts and pundits have blamed this attack partially on the fact that our country allowed its "human intelligence" capability to decline while relying more and more on satellite communications and technically oriented data collection.

Like the government, business and marketing executives have let their "consumer intelligence" slide too. In many cases, they have relied too heavily on factual point-of-purchase, real-time computer-generated-and-supplied data. They want to see the future, yet they ignore the very information—the consumer intelligence—that will enable them to see it. Why? Because it does not graph nicely and it requires a human being, an expensive intelligent one with some real-world experiences to process it, not a computer.

In this book, *Why People Buy Things They Don't Need*, you will gain insight and understanding about why consumers behave the way they do. By understanding the *why*, your business strategy will be grounded and supported by "consumer intelligence," not just data. You'll find lots of statistics here, but you will also discover a new way to look at your customers, not as points on a data graph, but as real, complex, irrational but strangely predictable, human beings who love and fear and strive and feel pain. They are wonderful. They are frustrating. They are awe-inspiring. They are fascinating. Moreover, they are our customers. We desperately need them. And we had better respect them. That is why you as a business and marketing executive need this book, because without the consumer your business disappears.

Chapter 1

WHY DO PEOPLE BUY THINGS THEY DON'T NEED?

Because they *do need!*

That is the simple answer to a profoundly challenging question. Consumers buy things to satisfy a concrete, distinctly felt need. Many consumer marketers go little further than this—uncover the need, target it in advertising, and voila, products get sold. But in today's diverse, networked, information-crowded marketplace, it is hard to rise above the background noise of commerce with practical, needs-based advertising.

What do any of us *really* need? More fundamentally, how do you reach a mass-consumer market where my need is so different from your need and your need is so different from that of each of your neighbors? What about where the need cannot be defined in conscious, rationally based criteria, but is ephemeral, based on emotions and feelings? Any psychologist will tell you that each of our individual needs extends so much deeper than the simple physical subsistence level. In today's consumer-driven society, satisfying consumer needs has less to do with the practical meeting of physical needs and everything to do with gratifying desires based upon emotions. *The act* of consuming, rather than *the item* being consumed, satisfies the need. That is the subject of this book.

WHAT DO CONTEMPORARY AMERICANS NEED?

Economists and social scientists who study the realm of consumer spending can tell us much about what consumers buy, where they buy it, when they buy, and how much they spend. They chart it, graph it, and measure it. However, the flood of numbers emanating from this research cannot reveal the "why" that ultimately drives consumer behavior. Yet, by understanding *the why*, practicing marketers can communicate with potential consumers to entice them to buy products using the emotionally based, right-brain inspired language.

The overall message of so many books that explore modern American consumerism is to shake their fingers at our wasteful consumer behavior and call on consumers to stop their unnecessary, throw-away spending. Think if Americans directed their economic might toward the public good and infrastructure, rather than the extravagant weekly, even daily, shopping trips to the malls, armed with credit cards and insatiable consumer appetites. For example, Juliet Schor, of Harvard University, writes: "The intensification of competitive spending has affected more than family finances. There is also a boomerang effect on the public purse and collective consumption. As the pressures on private spending have escalated, support for public goods and for paying taxes, has eroded. Education, social services, public safety, recreation, and culture are being squeezed. The deterioration of public goods then adds even more pressure to spend privately. People respond to inadequate public services by enrolling their children in private schools, buying security systems, and spending time at Discovery Zone rather than the local playground."

Yet, in light of the tragic events of September 11, 2001 and the worsening economic crisis, this point of view seems strangely un-American. The simple fact remains that our whole economic system, even our way of life, depends upon the continued, sustained practice of "excessive," as some see it, American consumerism.

ONCE A CONSUMER NATION, ALWAYS A CONSUMER NATION

As long as the U.S. Department of Commerce, under the Bureau of Economic Analysis, has tracked the nation's Gross Domestic Product, consumer spending has been the very underpinning of the economy. Consumers' insatiable appetite to buy has contributed between 60 and 70 percent of the GDP since 1929, with only a slight downturn to about 50 percent during the war years of the 1940s. In 1929, 1930, and 1940, personal consumption as a percentage of GDP topped 70 percent, demonstrating the long-standing foundational role consumer spending has played in the American economy.

PERSONAL CONSUMPTION

Expenditure as percent of GDP in $ billions

	GDP	Personal Consumption	Percent of Total Economy
1929	$103.7	$77.5	74.7%
1930	81.3	70.2	78.9
1940	101.3	71.2	70.3
1950	294.3	192.7	65.5
1960	527.4	323.3	63.0
1970	1,039.7	648.9	62.4
1980	2,795.6	1,762.9	63.1
1990	5,803.2	3,831.5	68.0
1995	7,400.5	4,969.0	67.1
1996	7,815.2	5,237.5	67.0
1997	8,318.4	5,528.3	66.5
1998	6,751.5	5,656.0	66.7
1999	9,288.6	8,250.2	67.4
2000	9,872.9	8,728.4	68.2

Source: U.S. Bureau of Economic Analysis

CONSUMERS SHIFT AWAY FROM NECESSITY–DRIVEN SPENDING

Consumer spending has kept the American economy afloat through-out the 20th century, but the way consumers spend their money has changed significantly over the past 70 years. Consumer-durable spending as a percentage of personal consumption expenditures has hovered in the range of 10 to 13 percent since 1929, with a slight peak in 1950 at 16 percent, but the share of consumer spending on non-durable goods and services has varied significantly. Non-durable spending includes such essential categories as food and clothing along with discretionary categories of gasoline, fuel oil, tobacco, toi-letries, semi-durable home furnishings, cleaning supplies, drugs and sundries, toys, stationery, magazines, newspapers, flowers, seeds, and potted plants. Non-durable spending accounted for as much as 51 percent of personal consumption expenditures in 1950 to as little as 30 percent in 2000. One reason for the significant decline is that essentials, i.e., food and clothing, now cost less relative to total income. In the later decades of the 20th century, essentials have cap-tured far less of the consumers' budget. In 1930, food alone com-prised nearly 26 percent of personal consumption expenditures, and

SPENDING ON DISCRETIONARY ITEMS

As a percentage of all personal consumption expenditures (PCE)

	1930	1940	1950	1960	1970	1980	1990	2000
Durables	**10.3**	**11.0**	**15.9**	**13.0**	**13.1**	**12.2**	**12.2**	**12.2**
Motor vehicles	3.1	3.9	7.1	5.9	5.5	4.9	5.4	5.2
Furniture	5.4	5.3	7.1	5.4	5.5	4.9	4.5	4.6
Other	1.6	1.5	1.7	1.7	2.1	2.3	2.3	2.5
Discretionary	4.7	5.4	8.8	7.6	7.6	7.2	7.7	7.7
Non-Durable	**48.4**	**6.0**	**51.0**	**46.0**	**41.9**	**39.5**	**32.5**	**29.6**
Food	25.6	28.4	28.0	24.8	22.2	20.2	16.6	14.2
Clothing and shoes	11.4	10.5	10.2	8.1	7.4	6.1	5.3	4.7
Gas and oil	4.7	5.3	4.6	4.8	4.1	5.8	3.1	2.7
Other	6.7	7.9	8.2	8.3	8.3	7.4	7.4	7.9
Discretionary	11.4	13.2	12.8	13.1	12.4	13.2	10.5	10.6
Services	**41.3**	**37.1**	**33.1**	**41.0**	**45.0**	**48.4**	**55.3**	**56.2**
Housing	16.0	13.6	11.3	14.5	14.5	14.5	15.3	14.3
House operations	5.6	5.6	4.9	6.1	5.8	6.5	5.9	5.7
Transportation	3.1	2.9	3.2	3.4	3.7	3.7	3.7	4.1
Medical care	3.3	3.2	3.7	5.3	7.8	10.3	14.1	14.8
Recreation	2.4	2.4	2.0	2.1	2.3	2.4	3.2	3.8
Other	11.0	9.1	7.9	9.6	10.9	11.0	13.1	15.6
Discretionary	16.5	14.4	13.1	15.1	15.9	17.1	20.0	23.5
Total Discretionary	**32.6**	**33.0**	**34.7**	**35.8**	**36.9**	**37.5**	**38.2**	**41.8**

Source: Bureau of Economic Analysis, NIPA tables

clothes took another 11 percent. Compare that 37 percent budgeted to essentials in 1930 with consumer spending in 2000 on the same necessities, where food (14 percent) and clothing (5 percent) together accounted for only 19 percent of total expenditures. Today, after consumers budget for essentials, they have a substantial amount of money left to spend on discretionary items.

In the current economy, the services category has captured share from other categories, especially consumer non-durable spending. Services include essentials such as housing, as well as discretionary expenses, such as recreation, education, transportation, and many household operations. Various personal services such as legal, payments to financial institutions, donations to religious and welfare groups, and foreign travel are also included in the discretionary spending for services. In 1940, services made up only one-third of consumer spending, while in 2000 services rose to a startling 59 percent, an increase of 26 percentage points.

Another category of spending that most contemporary Americans would call an essential expenditure is medical care. In 2000, medical care accounted for more consumer spending, 14.8 percent, than did housing, with a 14.3 percent share. Of all spending categories, medical care has increased the most since 1930, when it represented only 3.3 percent of personal consumption expenditures.

TODAY, OVER 40 PERCENT OF CONSUMER SPENDING IS DISCRETIONARY

While one can convincingly argue that a significant share of medical care is discretionary in nature, for purposes of this exploration we consider medical care, housing, and household operations essential expenditures in the services category. In the non-durable category, we categorize food and clothing as essential. Finally, among durables, we classify only spending on furniture and household equipment as essential, though, like medical care, a significant portion of spending in that category is discretionary in nature. Excluding consumer spending that is allocated to essentials, over 30 percent of consumer spending in 2000, or $2,812.5 billion, was discretionary spending. That is more than gross private domestic investment ($1,767.5 billion) and government consumption expenditures and gross investment ($1,741 billion), the other two segments that make up the national Gross Domestic Product.

UNDERSTANDING THE DISCRETIONARY SPENDING EQUATION OR WHAT YOU WILL LEARN FROM READING THIS BOOK

In sum, consumers and their discretionary spending—on wants, not needs—make a surprisingly large contribution to the nation's overall economy. If consumer marketers can harness the power of Americans' need to consume, they can gain market share, build brand recognition, and increase profitability. In later chapters, we will explore the "whys" that propel consumers in their search for emotional satisfaction through the things they buy. We will also examine distinctions among four types of consumer discretionary spending, and how the consumer perceives each. The types of discretionary spending include:

> ***Pragmatic***—this covers discretionary purchases that people don't necessarily need, but which they perceive as making their lives better in meaningful, measurable ways. Usually, these purchases have a practical or functional component. Consumers will often leap from what is considered an essential purchase to a more highly discretionary one, thus spending more money and gaining more emotional satisfaction from the purchase.

> ***Indulgences***—These are life's little luxuries that consumers can buy without guilt. Primarily, they bring emotional satisfaction to the consumer by being frivolous, somewhat extravagant, but not so expensive that the consumer feels remorse.

> ***Lifestyle Luxuries***—Luxuries are "more" than is needed. Lifestyle luxuries have a practical aspect to their purchase, such as a car, a pen, fine china, or a watch. While they fulfill a practical need, lifestyle luxuries are a quantum leap beyond the basic item needed to effectively serve the essential purpose.

> ***Aspirational Luxuries***—Unlike lifestyle luxuries, which have a practical component, aspirational luxuries are purchased largely for the pure joy that owning them brings, such as original art, antiques and vintage collectibles, boats and yachts, and fine jewelry. As with lifestyle luxuries, aspirational luxuries usually are tied to a "Brand." When consumers buy aspirational luxuries, they are making a statement about themselves—who they are, their aspirations, and what they stand for.

Through research, we will delve into the purchase incidence for 30 different categories of discretionary purchases—what consumers look for in these purchases, and what they get out of making them.

As we probe discretionary purchases, we discover that in order for consumers to buy things they don't need, they use justifiers as excuses and reasons that give them permission to buy. Some consumers and some purchases need more powerfully charged justifiers, while other consumers and purchases require little in the way of an excuse to buy something not needed. Sometimes these justifiers are fairly mundane; other times they are elaborate fantasies consumers conjure up to give them license to make the desired purchase. We have identified 14 distinct justifiers consumers combine and manipulate to give them the permission they need to buy.

We'll also explore how consumers' need for discretionary purchases impacts their shopping behavior, such as where they shop, how they research the planned purchases, and how they discover new things that will satisfy unfulfilled emotional needs.

Finally, as we build our understanding of the emotionally motivated consumer, the ultimate goal is for marketers to learn innovative ways to apply their new insights into dynamic, fresh marketing strategies. Marketers can use these insights to position their products strategically along the discretionary purchase continuum, playing to the various justifiers that consumers use to make a discretionary purchase. Throughout this book, we will bring the discussion back from the conceptual to the practical by profiling outstanding marketers and the best marketing practices that help them sell more things that people don't *need*, but *want*.

Chapter 2

WHAT DO WE NEED? MORE THAN YOU EVER IMAGINED

America is one of the wealthiest countries in the world. A typical middle-class, even lower class, American cannot even imagine what life is like for the typical citizen of Afghanistan, Zimbabwe, or Indonesia. Our standard of living far exceeds any other developed nation. What we take for granted as an essential part of our way of life—unlimited electricity, clean running water, refrigeration, and television—is far beyond the means of a significant portion of the world's population. Worldwide, the average per capita gross national product is currently about $7,200. The United States per capita of $36,200 is five times as large. With U.S. median household income just under $40,000 and median net worth of $71,600, the average American's wealth is unimaginable for most of the world's inhabitants.

WHAT AMERICANS NEED TO LIVE

When talking about what we need, as opposed to what we want, it is important to account for our contemporary American standard of living. More than two-thirds of U.S. householders own their own home. They live in a median-sized home of about 1,700 square feet divided into 5 or 6 rooms. The typical home is on a one-third acre lot, giving the typical American household some "breathing room." Almost every American home (99.4 percent) has some kind of heating source and almost every one (98.5 percent) has a complete bathroom, including toilet, sink, and bathtub. Moreover, not all of the 1.5 percent of households without a complete bathroom live this way out of necessity.

GROSS DOMESTIC PRODUCT PER CAPITA

For selected countries, 2000

$36,200 and above	United States, Luxembourg
$25,000-$36,199	Austria, Belgium, Denmark, Hong Kong, Norway, Singapore, Switzerland
$20,000-$24,999	Australia, Canada, Finland, France, Germany, Ireland, Italy, Japan, Netherlands, Qatar, Sweden, United Arab Emirates, United Kingdom
$15,000-$19,999	Argentina, Bahrain, Greece, Israel, Kuwait, New Zealand, Portugal, Spain, South Korea, Taiwan
$10,000-$14,999	Chile, Czech Republic, Estonia, Hungary, Malaysia, Martinique, Slovenia
$7,200	Worldwide average
$5,000-$9,999	Algeria, Botswana, Brazil, Bulgaria, Colombia, Croatia, Guadeloupe, Iran, Lebanon, Mexico, Poland, Romania, Russia, Thailand, South Africa, Turkey, Uruguay
$1,000-$4,999	Albania, Angola, Bangladesh, Belize, Bolivia, Burma, Cambodia, Cameroon, Chad, China, Cuba, Ecuador, Egypt, Guatemala, Guyana, Haiti, Honduras, India, Indonesia, Iraq, Jamaica, Jordan, Kenya, North Korea, Kyrgyzstan, Liberia, Mongolia, Morocco, Mozambique, Namibia, Nicaragua, Pakistan, Paraguay, Peru, Philippines, Senegal, Sri Lanka, Swaziland, Syria, Tajikistan, Uganda, Ukraine, Uzbekistan, Vietnam, Yugoslavia, Zimbabwe
Under $1,000	Afghanistan, Congo Republic, Ethiopia, Madagascar, Nigeria, Rwanda, Somalia, Zambia

Source: The World Factbook, CIA, 2001

Some religious groups, such as the Amish, choose to live without indoor plumbing and other modern conveniences.

As for the modern conveniences that grace the typical American home, a majority of American households owns a car; only 17 percent live without this symbol of American freedom. The majority also have air conditioning in their homes. Most own a clothes washer and dryer, have an automatic dishwasher, ceiling fan, microwave oven, range and oven, frost-free refrigerator, water heater, stereo equipment, color television, VCR, cordless phone, and answering machine.

The simple fact is the contemporary American lives so far above subsistence, we have lost touch with basic needs of life: food for nutrition, basic clothing, and shelter for warmth and protection. Many people in other countries of the world live dangerously close to subsistence and know the pangs of hunger and the chill of weather with-

AMERICAN WAY OF LIFE

Wealth:

Median net worth $71,600

Median household income . . . $38,885

Homeownership rate . . . 66.8% (1999)

Housing (1997)

Median number of rooms: 5.3

If owner occupied 6.1

Median square footage 1,685

Heating equipment 99.4%

Complete bathrooms:

None 1.5%

1 only 46%

2 or more 52%

Single units or mobile homes . . . 74%

Median lot size . . . . 0.33 acres

Amenities (Owner Occupied)

Porch, deck, balcony, or patio . . . 85%

Usable fireplace 42%

Separate dining room 48%

2 or more living/recreation rooms . . 48%

Garage/carport 73%

Cars:

None 17%

1 car 48%

2 or more cars 35%

Household Appliances:

Air conditioner:

Central 46.8%

Room 24.8%

Clothes washer 77.4%

Clothes dryer 71.2%

Dishwasher 50.2%

Ceiling fan 60.1%

Freezer 33.2%

Microwave oven 83.0%

Oven 98.8%

Self-cleaning oven 44.1%

Range 99.2%

Refrigerator 99.8%

Frostfree refrigerator 86.8%

Water heater 100.0%

Stereo equipment 68.8%

Color TV 98.7%

1 only 31.8%

2 or more 66.9%

VCR 88.0%

Personal computers 35.1%

Cordless phone 61.4%

Answering machine 58.4%

*Source: U.S. Statistical Abstract, Appliances and office equipment
used by households, 1997; Housing units and lot, 1999*

out the benefit of adequate clothing and shelter. While most Americans today enjoy a higher standard of living, it has not always been so. During the Colonial period and the Civil War, among other times, Americans were also deprived, but they valued their freedom more than material goods. Americans have also faced deprivation in war and during the Depression. Generations born before World War II share cultural memories of living "without" and "in need." The generations that went before were the keepers of family traditions and passed down practical knowledge about living frugally.

However, today's baby boomers and their children are rapidly losing touch with this shared cultural memory of hardship. Boomers and younger generations know nothing about getting along before cars, indoor plumbing, and antibiotics. The generations that were born and came of age after the last World War know little about doing without, struggling to put food on the table, stretching a dollar, and delayed gratification. Spoiled the younger generations may be, but they are the consumers who express their wants, desires, and dreams in terms of needs and necessities because they have never done without.

MAJOR APPLIANCES ARE NECESSITIES OF CONTEMPORARY AMERICAN LIFE

Before moving into an exploration of the things people buy that they do not "need," we will first examine a category that most Americans view as a necessity—major household appliances. A focus group participant explains the decision-making process that she and her husband went through to decide between buying a refrigerator or an entertainment center for the new home they are building:

> *Our most recent purchase of something we didn't "need" was an entertainment center. We already have one, but we are building a brand new house and we wanted something new for the house. Now that we are building, things are tight. We could have used the entertainment center we had, but we decided to buy a new one and move the old one into another room. There are other things we need for the home, like a refrigerator. The entertainment center could have been put on hold, but it was one of those things...we were in the right place at the right time. We went a little bit over what we needed in an entertainment center in terms of price. We upgraded the wood, so the price went up. It was an opportunistic purchase.*

For this homeowner, a refrigerator is a 'necessity,' required for this family to maintain its way of life. With money tight and the couple struggling to balance the demands of building a new home while maintaining the current one, their decision to buy a "luxury"—a new entertainment center—rather than the necessity is inexplicable. In buying the entertainment center, they even went over their budget by ordering the center in a more expensive wood. They realize that they did not need to buy a new entertainment center, but purchasing the center gave this couple so much more pleasure and satisfaction than buying a new refrigerator. Lying under the surface of her story is a realization. The couple believes they will always have enough money to satisfy their need for the basics, i.e., refrigerator. However, when confronted with deciding between purchasing a luxury and buying a necessity, they go for the purchase that is compelling and emotionally satisfying. Need can wait, because it will always be satisfied, but want and desire drive purchases, since you never know when you will find exactly what you long for.

> **Need can wait, but want and desire drive purchases.**

MAJOR APPLIANCE RETAILERS AND MARKETERS CAN LEARN FROM PEOPLE BUYING THINGS THEY DON'T NEED

Retailers and marketers of major appliances can learn much about selling necessities from knowing more about the reasons people buy things they *don't* need. First, let us recognize the two reasons why people buy appliances: to replace a worn-out appliance and to equip a newly built home. Industry marketers perceive housing starts as the major opportunity since a single housing start generates sales of five to eight major appliances, whereas replacement purchases tend to be limited to a single appliance. Practical considerations, product features and benefits, are the primary drivers for sales of a particular item, but price, credit terms, and conditions also play a role. Brand is also important in the purchase decision as it carries a quality and reliability message. Consumers who have had a satisfactory experience with one brand in the past are already inclined toward the same brand in subsequent purchases.

Marketing strategist, Sergio Zyman, known for his years as brand executive for Coca-Cola, provides the best definition of marketing, in his book, *The End of Marketing as We Know It*: "Marketing is how to sell more things to more people more often for more money." Major appliance retailers, manufacturers, and marketers will sell more major appliances to more people more often for more money by turning their products from a necessity into a "desirable" that provides not just essential functionality but emotional satisfaction. The remainder of this chapter explains how they can do just that.

Fashion—Take the ordinary and make it extraordinary

The nation's major-appliance companies tend to be run by male executives who rise from engineering, manufacturing, and other technical backgrounds. Intuitive fashion sense just does not spring naturally from the corridors of power in the major-appliance industry. With focus on product features, energy efficiency, saving time, and cost-effectiveness, the industry is left-brain dominated. Its approach to marketing: Put a chart outlining the features of the product on the front of the machine and, *voila,* the customer is sold. This just does not cut it with the target market for these products—women.

> **"The chief aim of marketing is to sell more things to more people more often for more money."**
> **—Sergio Zyman**

Women are attuned to fashion as well as performance. They want products that look good while they do their job to perfection. They take superior performance for granted. They expect every frost-free refrigerator from the lowest to the highest priced to keep their food cold and safe. However, the refrigerator that performs its basic function in style is the one that she wants to have and use in her kitchen.

Fashion takes the ordinary and makes it extraordinary. Manufacturers that produce appliances that look good can charge more for their products. As car manufacturers and fashion designers have known for years, the introduction of new styles and designs sends consumers to the store to buy the latest design. How difficult can it be for major appliance companies to incorporate a fashion or design sensibility into their new product lines? Greater profits will result when appliance manufacturers pay as much attention to the outside as they do to the inside of their products.

Major-appliance manufacturers need to cross-pollinate their organizations with executives who bring training and experience in fashion and design. These kinds of people may not "fit" naturally into the existing organizational structure. There may well be a culture clash,

Getting It Right

JENN-AIR
Style and performance in kitchen appliances for aspirers

Within Maytag's corporate family of brands, Jenn-Air is distinguished by its 100-percent commitment to cooking and the kitchen. It is also the most exclusive, top-tier brand for Maytag, hardly a shirker when it comes to premium home brands. If Maytag is a premium brand in home appliances, how is Jenn-Air distinguished and differentiated? Susan Fisher, director of marketing for the Jenn-Air brand, explains that it all starts with design. "The Jenn-Air brand is largely defined by innovative style along with distinctive product features. Jenn-Air invented a new way of cooking with its downdraft, indoor-grilling cooktops. And convection is standard in its ovens. Jenn-Air stands for style and performance in the kitchen. While Maytag offers kitchen appliances, its Maytag brand is founded upon laundry products and its kitchen appliances are more basic than Jenn-Air. Features that are standard in Jenn-Air are often add-ons for Maytag."

The target market for Jenn-Air appliances couldn't be more distinct. Its core customers have a passion for cooking. They recognize the "badge value" of the Jenn-Air name and what it says about the owner as a cook. Buyers tend to be affluent homeown-ers who seek exclusivity in the brands they use in their home. A Jenn-Air kitchen is not positioned for the first-time homebuyer, but for the trade-up buyer or home remodeler. "Some 90 percent of Jenn-Air purchases involve a hammer or saw," Fisher says. "Our appliances are mainly custom-installed, so we touch a totally different consumer market than other appliance makers who specialize in simple "plug-in" installation. When customers buy a Jenn-Air, they are often involved in a three-month, or longer, process of design, including selection of kitchen cabinets, floor and wall coverings, and so on. Dreamers and aspirers want this brand in their home."

With its position as a more exclusive brand, Jenn-Air appliances cost more, owing to their higher capital and research and development costs. While they cost more, they also deliver higher profit margins back to the company. For Maytag, Jenn-Air's style is a good investment.

With Jenn-Air's exclusive focus on cooking appliances and other kitchen appliances that support the cooking process, such as refrigerators and dish-washers, they have more specialized distribution and marketing strategies than Maytag. While some Maytag dealers also carry Jenn-Air, the brand's focus on custom installation means that designers, architects, and home builders often influence the purchase decision, so Jenn-Air directs marketing campaigns to these trades. While Maytag advertises almost exclusively on television, Jenn-Air devotes its advertising budget to print media, especially epicurean, home design, and shelter magazines. "When someone is designing a new house or remodeling, they tend to buy all these titles. They clip out pictures of kitchens they like and build a file. Jenn-Air wants to be in that file when it's turned over to the designer," Fisher explains. "Our customers see Jenn-Air as a central part of the kitchen they always dreamed of owning. It's a move up and a step up in quality, design, and performance."

How does Jenn-Air stay ahead of its customers' aspirations in new cooking technology? "Jenn-Air is committed to continual research," Fisher says. "Market research for us is a continual process. We do research at every step in the process from concept development to product delivery. We are especially attuned to consumers' needs in kitchen-shopping and cooking practices. We go into their homes to study their behavior and go with them while they are shopping for appliances to observe their unarticulated needs. And there is style research—we do lots of style research."

Putting all that research to work in dreaming up new kitchen appliances for the aspirational market is a business unit composed of more women than men. "Maytag as a company has lots of women on its team," Fisher explains. "Since we are so involved with products that make women's lives better, female executives, managers, and designers bring an intuitive understanding of what the woman consumer wants and values. In the Jenn-Air business unit, women tend to predominate, not by design; they were hired as the best person for the job." Yet today's upscale appliance marketplace is becoming more attuned to men, she adds. " Interestingly when it comes to buying Jenn-Air, men tend to be more involved with this decision, largely because men are more engaged in the design-and-build process. We also see more men than ever cooking and using the kitchen, so men represent a key growth market segment for our brand," Fisher concludes.

but staffing for design expertise from outside the industry will go far to infuse major-appliance companies with fresh ideas that will transform their products from purely functional boxes into home-fashion statements.

Avoid mediocrity in new products—Ignore the competition, get close to the customer

In many highly competitive industries today, corporations tend to expend considerable time, money, and human resources on competitive tracking, monitoring, and otherwise "keeping up with the Joneses." This is especially true in major appliances, where the top five manufacturers account for more than 95 percent of all core-appliance sales such as refrigerators, dishwashers, and washing machines. While these manufacturers have their eyes focused on the competition, they too frequently fall out of touch with their existing consumer markets, their potential markets, and the trends, changes, and factors that are influencing the future of the market. In too many industries, competitive analysis is the "poor-man's" substitute for market research. Companies dedicated to competitive research assume that their competitors are doing the time-consuming, hard, and costly job of consumer research. They spend their time watching the competition and the new product releases, analyzing products and features, so they can piggyback on others' efforts.

This approach to new product development is a guarantee of product mediocrity as the cycle of competitor-copying-competitor turns back on itself in an endless loop. I cut my teeth professionally in the field of competitive analysis and even belonged to the Society for Competitive Intelligence Professionals for a time. However, I came to realize that the end of this competitive analysis and tracking work was me-too marketing strategies. The simple fact is that competitive analysis work is easy. Corporate executives are highly skilled at reading balance sheets and SEC filings and deriving insight into competitive strategy and tactics. It is a realm where executives feel comfortable. They understand the inner workings of other executives' minds and thus other companies' behavior and strategies. However, expose these same executives to the vagaries, conflicting information, and "hocus-pocus" of consumer market research and they are out of their element entirely. If you can't chart it, graph it, or table it, they do not want to deal with it.

Every industry that creates products for the consumer market should cross-pollinate with fashion and design experts. These industries must also invest time, money, and powerful corporate resources to understand their consumer markets better. It is not enough to bring a few consumers into a lab to test new products. They need to explore how their company's products improve customers' lives and what makes their hearts flutter when they talk about stoves, refrigerators, and washing machines. Appliance industry executives need to get beyond the left-brain-dominant product features of their appliances. They need to study how customers really decide which brand to buy, what the brand means to them, and how it reflects upon their identities and value systems. Male-dominated industries selling technical, e.g. male-oriented, products to female-dominated consumer markets face a disconnect. Taking superior features and quality for granted, women don't bring a product-and-features left-brain orientation to the store when they shop for appliances. However, if an appliance also looks good, is the right color, and is a brand that enables her to express herself, that is the one she will buy.

> **Every industry that creates products for the consumer should cross-pollinate with fashion and design experts.**

If you sell to women, then *SELL* to women

Retailing of major appliances is totally at odds with the way people shop, especially women. Even worse, with few exceptions, the way major appliances are sold at retail has not changed since the early 1960s when I accompanied my parents to buy a new refrigerator. I know it has not changed since the first time I shopped for a major appliance for myself in the 1980s. No wonder that Circuit City has gotten out of the major appliance business and American Appliance has gone under completely. The retailing of major appliances is long overdue for an overhaul.

Recently, I was a customer for a major appliance. My dishwasher was leaking all over the kitchen floor and the repairman sent out from our local appliance store said it would cost just about as much to fix it as to buy a new one. With that suggestion, I went off to the store to buy a new dishwasher.

When you enter a major appliance store, everything is so logically arranged. Along this wall, the refrigerators are all lined up. Over there is every variation of electric and gas stoves. Running up the middle are the washers, and on the back side of the aisle are the dryers. In one corner, stacked one on top of the other, are the dishwashers. Seemingly on every couple of items, a sale sign is prominently displayed—"$50 off" here and "Only $199" there. When I told the salesman that the repairman sent me in, he took me right over to the dishwasher display and proceeded to bore me with a recitation of each brand's features, which were all the same to me. How did I decide? I picked a quiet one, priced just under the most expensive model, that was also available in black, like my last one. After we set up an appointment for delivery, I left the store knowing I had solved my dishwasher issue, and the salesman was happy to have made the sale.

The problem? This whole experience was totally wrong. I went into the store with a "need," e.g. my dishwasher broke and I needed a new one. However, I had a significant "desire" that went undiscovered by the salesman, so the store did not profit, and I was ultimately dissatisfied. A little probing on the salesman's part would have uncovered the fact that my dishwasher was purchased, along with all my other kitchen appliances, about ten years ago when we built our house. In the life of a major appliance, ten years is a magic number. It is long enough so that the existing appliances feel "old." The homeowner can justify upgrading all the appliances in the name of energy savings, compelling new features, or getting a good deal on a whole set of new kitchen appliances. The summer before my dishwasher broke, my husband and I invested in new paint for the living room, dining room and kitchen, and refinished the hardwood floors throughout. With all these upgrades, I had been thinking seriously about replacing the stove. A new side-by-side refrigerator would certainly be welcome, now that my two sons are hitting their teen years with the resulting appetites.

The simple fact: there was nothing about my major appliance buying trip that excited me, or pulled me in to the fun of picking out a brand new kitchen. With all the appliances lined up one after the other and arranged by type, not how I would use them in my kitchen, they all looked the same—big boxes with labels on them. In that barren setting, I could not envision what my kitchen would look like, or how I would feel cooking with brand new appliances. While my stated need was satisfied, my desire definitely was not. It would have

---

Prescription for Major Appliance Retailing
- Display appliances in room settings with matching appliances and cabinetry to encourage consumer fantasies
- Fewer models, better presentation to "romance" the buyer
- Offer multiple-product package pricing with financing
- One-stop remodeling offering appliances, cabinets, countertops, and installation

---

taken so little effort on the part of the appliance store salesman to turn my $400 purchase into a $2,500 investment.

If I ran a major appliance store, the first thing I would do is get rid of the row upon row of appliance boxes. I would carve out lovely little rooms to feature all the different types and styles of appliances. There would be a gourmet-style kitchen here with the latest stainless designs, and a starter kitchen there with simple cabinetry and basic appliances. There would be a top-of-the-line country kitchen with retro-appliances, and a to-die-for laundry room with a folding counter and shelves for all the soap powders and cleaning equipment. Men may like to shop with products lined up for comparison, but women want to dream and fantasize. They want to see what the appliances would be like in their own home. I would price the appliances by grouping with a nice discount on the purchase of two or three matching ones. To equip my store with these wonderful room settings, I would work out a strategic alliance with a home remodeling or cabinetry service. I would get into the business of selling not just appliance boxes, but fully equipped, custom-designed kitchens and laundry rooms.

A store set up like this would have overcome the ineptitude of the salesman with whom I dealt. Rather than take me to the sterile dishwasher display, he would have escorted me into my "dream kitchen." It would not have taken me long to have him writing up my order for three major appliances and a new countertop to boot. I did not mention that a countertop is also on my "desire" list.

Sadly though, I do not have a wonderful new kitchen. It is entirely too much work for me today to go out and buy a new stove and refrigerator. Dealing with an appliance salesman once in a year is about as much as I can handle. I do not have a clue where I can get new countertops or what kind I want, since there are so many choices

today. I do not know how difficult or easy it would be to have someone come in and install them. I am too busy to undertake this project
right now. Although I'd like a new kitchen and I can afford a new
kitchen, I can get by without it. After all, everything still works.

This experience illustrates a fundamental law of consumer dynamics: A consumer in motion stays in motion; a consumer at rest stays at
rest. That is, it is easier to persuade a consumer that is actively in the
market to buy more, than to persuade one to buy who is not participating in the marketplace. The appliance retailer's best opportunity to
sell more appliances is at that moment when the consumer has overcome inertia and wants to make a purchase. Unfortunately, my retailer
missed this wonderful opportunity by selling me only what I needed
rather than all that I wanted. My retailer did not understand how to
turn wants into needs. And, that is what the rest of this book is about.

Chapter 3

IF CONSUMER SPENDING IS THE ENGINE OF THE ECONOMY, THEN DISCRETIONARY SPENDING IS THE "GAS"

As we have seen, consumer spending drives the U.S. economy. Moreover, consumers' desire for things they want, but don't need, is the lure that draws them to the stores, the mall, and now the internet. The strong emotional gratification that consumers gain from their discretionary purchases is the reward that reinforces continued purchases of things desired, but not needed. Like Pavlov's dogs, they seek that same level of gratification repeatedly. A focus group respondent explained her experience buying things she doesn't need: "Essentials are things you need, but you also need a little 'fluff,' not all substance. Just buying essentials is boring, so you need to buy things that are frivolous to make life less boring. It makes you feel better."

What is the source of gratification? Is it achieved through the act of shopping for something not needed or gratification from the object itself? Evidence points to both as important contributors to consumer satisfaction. In planning a new purchase, consumers often develop elaborate fantasies surrounding their search, finding it, and making it their own. As another focus group participant explained about the recent purchase of a car bought for pleasure, not need: "Anticipation is everything. Everything you do, you anticipate. That is the fun, and that is part of who you are. By anticipating something new, you are trying to level things out [e.g., keep your emotions level]. You go on one vacation, and before that is over, you are already planning your next vacation. You get satisfaction, and you are so thrilled you start planning the next purchase. Satisfaction sets up more anticipation. You can't wait to do it again. Anticipation is stress, healthy stress. You are still enjoying the satisfaction you got and anticipating the next time." Another respondent adds, "You can anticipate little things, like taking a bath when you buy soap powders; buying fuzzy slippers to come home and put on after work; or going out to a really nice restaurant." In the act of consuming, these consumers act out vignettes and fantasies—sometimes small, sometimes very elaborate—that may well provide more satisfaction than the actual experience of shopping and buying the item.

In shopping, the search for a desired item encourages consumers' fantasies, allowing them to create more complex tableaus in which to act out their dreams and desires. Another recent new-car buyer explained: "The search for something adds to the anticipation. In shopping for my car, I spent time thinking about what kind of car I wanted. I had fun going to dealers, playing one against the other. I found a thrill in the search. When I finally picked the car and bought it, I almost felt a letdown. The search was over. Now that I got what I wanted, I have to pay for it." Once the purchase cycle is completed, reality sets in. Inevitably though, a new shopping fantasy will begin to brew as the consumer starts a new cycle of anticipation and searching, leading to purchase, then followed by letdown.

> **The consumer's feelings often may have more to do with the act of purchasing than with the object.**

Some consumers gain satisfaction from developing a shopping fantasy they can act out. For others, it is the power they feel from finding something and being able to buy it. Interestingly, the consumer's feelings often may have more to do with the act of purchasing than with the object that the shopper buys. In response to the description of the thrill of the hunt, another respondent explains, "If you are an impulse shopper, you don't have any of that. There is no search, no anticipation. For me, the search can drive me crazy. I like to buy. I see something; I find it; I buy it. I like to know that I am the one who got it. For me, it's the power I feel when I buy. I am a big impulse shopper. I like to buy, not to think about it."

CONSUMERS UNDER STRESS

After the terrorist attack on September 11, 2001, the American consumer landscape changed, perhaps forever. Along with the loss of our illusion of safety from acts of war carried out on our soil, went consumer confidence and the feeling of well-being that consuming brought to Americans. Today, confronting an uncertain future, threatened by terrorist acts of horror at home, with our troops committed to military action overseas, American consumers face a crisis that our leaders warn us may extend over the next ten years.

Consumers in crisis are consumers under stress. Men and women react differently to stress. While men may seek out buddies in bars and at athletic games, women may go shopping. As we have uncovered in our research, emotional needs, not physical ones, drive a substantial amount of U.S. household spending. In the face of crisis, women who do the bulk of American households' shopping may spend more money on discretionary purchases to relieve stress and help them achieve emotional satisfaction. In our post 9/11 world, consumer marketers operating in every segment of the U.S. economy need to understand how consumers use shopping and buying things for emotional gratification and of achieving psychological well being. This emotionally driven consumption is the realm of discretionary spending.

DISCRETIONARY PRODUCT MATRIX DESCRIBES WHAT PEOPLE BUY THAT THEY DON'T NEED

Two lines or continuums can be used to define discretionary spending. The vertical continuum runs from necessities (e.g., food, clothing, and shelter) to the most extravagant purchases (e.g., things that you do not need). The horizontal continuum spans the range from physical, material comforts to emotional gratification resulting from buying something you don't need, but want. Within the matrix defined by these two continua reside the purchases of four different categories of discretionary purchases: Utilitarian, Indulgences, Lifestyle Luxuries, and Aspirational Luxuries.

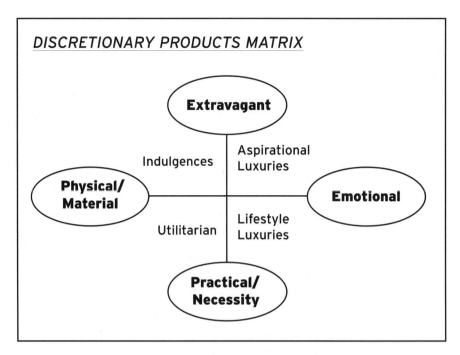

DISCRETIONARY PRODUCTS MATRIX

Utilitarian Purchase: Products that consumers do not strictly need but that will make their lives better in some measurable, physical way. [Examples include products that help you clean better, save time, or do something you are otherwise not able to do, such as blenders, rotisserie ovens, bread machines, food processors, microwave ovens, water purifiers, and so forth. Focus is on the practical.]

Lifestyle Luxuries: Brands essentially define all luxury purchases. Practical luxuries offer utility and usefulness, along with the prestige, image, and superior quality conferred by the brand. [Practical luxuries include automobiles (e.g., Mercedes, BMW); designer clothes (Gucci, Chanel); decorator furniture; watches (e.g., Rolex); gourmet appliances (Jenn-Air); and fine tabletop (e.g., Reidel, Waterford, and Wedgwood).]

Indulgences: Life's little luxuries that you can indulge in without guilt. Gratification is primarily emotional.[Examples include candles, lotions and potions to pamper yourself in the bath, cosmetics, costume jewelry, contemporary collectibles and figurines, gourmet chocolates, fresh flowers, perfume, entertainment products, games, videos, books, and crafts and hobbies.]

Aspirational Luxuries: Along with indulgences, aspirational luxuries satisfy primarily emotional needs. Through their purchases, consumers can express themselves, their value systems, their interests, and their passions. [The satisfaction derived is primarily emotional, rather than practical, for example, when buying original art, antiques and vintage collectibles, boats and yachts, and fine jewelry.]

This matrix universally describes discretionary spending for American consumers at every income level and lifestage. Yet points along the continuum are established by an individual's unique and personal value system—what one holds dear, what can easily be done without, what is affordable, and what one is willing to make sacrifices to attain. The continuum that defines what is a necessity and what is a frivolous expense is fluid, yet distinct, for each individual and different at each lifestage as the person evolves and changes.

VALUES GOVERN CONSUMER SPENDING

What one person calls a lifestyle luxury another might call a utilitarian purchase. What may be an indulgence for one is an aspirational luxury for someone else. Where a particular purchase fits in the discretionary product matrix is dependent upon many variables, not the least of which are income, lifestage, age, gender, and where the consumer lives. Even more individualistic is the individual's value system, passion, and identity.

> **A person's value system influences purchase decisions.**

An automobile purchase is highly dependent upon demographic factors. For example, if a person lives in a rural area, owning a car may be an absolute necessity, whereas for the city dweller who is well served by modern mass-transit systems, a car probably falls into the discretionary realm. Discretion also plays a role in what type of car to buy. Do you buy a new car or a used car? Do you buy a sedan, wagon, two-door, four-door, SUV, pickup truck, or four-wheel drive? Do you buy a Ford, Lincoln, Chevrolet, Cadillac, Honda, Lexus, Mercedes, Land Rover, or BMW? Who you are; where you live; your age, gender, and income; whether you have children; and what your friends drive all play a role in the decision that goes into purchasing a car.

Beyond demographics, a person's value system influences purchase decisions, as this respondent describes: "I don't need a Mercedes. I think a Mercedes is more than you need to get you from one place to another. It's about our belief system, which we talk about with our kids. We have tension there. On the one hand, we are embarrassed by what we have compared to some of our friends. On the other, some of my kids' friends get something and our kids come home and

Getting It Right

RONCO INVENTIONS:
Life transformation through a small kitchen appliance

Ron Popeil, founder of Ronco Inventions, has been called the "salesman of the century," and a study of his latest infomercial for the Showtime Rotisserie Grill is clear proof why. Working without an apparent script, Ron presents his Showtime Grill as a kitchen appliance described by one owner in the infomercial audience as a rotisserie that "has changed my life."

The infomercial is a tutorial in marketing and selling utilitarian products that nobody really needs. Through a simple presentation of information, supported with demonstrations and testimonials from audience members, Ron repeatedly drives home his message that owning the Showtime Grill will truly transform your life, not just the way you cook chicken. He breaks down the product-positioning message into a few essential components: easy

say, 'Why can't we get this?' That brand [Mercedes] is not me. I don't have that lifestyle. Some people do, but I don't."

Let's look more closely at how a consumer's value system, her individualized judgment, and her self-identity influence her perception of her own discretionary spending.

UTILITARIAN PURCHASES ARE DISTINGUISHED BY USEFULNESS

In the matrix, utilitarian purchases are high in physical gratification and low in extravagance. These extras in life offer some materially measurable benefit or improvement to the consumer. Functionality and practicality play an essential part, usually allowing the consumer to do something that could not be done before. Implicit in the definition of the discretionary utilitarian purchase is the concept of a trade-up from the necessary to the improved, more highly functioning utilitarian item. One respondent expressed it this way: "My latest discretionary purchase was a steam vacuum cleaner. I didn't strictly need it, but I wasn't spoiling myself in buying it. It cost a good amount of money, but I will use it. And it will save in the long run

to use, wonderful food, and high quality. His infomercial co-host reinforces the message, and his audience members, including regular people and professional chefs, underscore the same essential message. Through this presentation, the viewer sees and believes how everyone in the audience has changed their lives through the purchase and use of the Showtime Grill. It is a magnificent job of showing how a simple kitchen appliance can transform people's lives.

The positioning strategy for the grill combines product features with product benefits. However, what sells the grill is neither features nor benefits. It is the life-transforming value the grill bestows on the owner.

because I don't have to call someone to come into my house and clean the carpets."

Consumers say they achieve a feeling of well being from the purchase of these life-enhancing objects. Call it empowered ownership. As compared with buying a service to perform a similar function—say a carpet cleaning business to steam the carpets—consumers prefer ownership of the means or the tools (e.g. the steam vacuum) that will allow them to achieve their goal. Here is how one consumer explained her purchase decisions: "Products are easier and more convenient than services. Services require another person and are not so readily affordable. Once you do services, they are gone. Products last and last, and you don't have to depend on another person to get satisfaction from them. Product gives immediate satisfaction. And you can't really measure the quality of services. If you pay double for a haircut, do you really get double the quality? Service is less consistent."

Being able to "do-it-yourself" is a powerful motivator in the purchase of a utilitarian product. Suddenly you can achieve things you never could achieve before. You are more accomplished, more productive, and have more time and money to spend on other things. Your spouse, children, friends, and neighbors will admire you. You will achieve a new sense of self-fulfillment, confidence, and self-actualization. In other words, you'll be a winner.

Let's look more closely at how Ronco Inventions sells its rotisserie machine using a 30-minute infomercial. It is brilliant marketing because when you acquire the rotisserie machine, you get so much more than a machine that cooks good-tasting and healthful chicken. You become more in the know, more capable, more resourceful, a "superior" human being.

SELL MORE UTILITARIAN PRODUCTS

SELLING TIP: *Go beyond product features and benefits to life-transforming attributes: Create fantasies and show how product fulfills them.*

Many products are sold solely on product features (e.g., this blender blends better than the other blender) and benefits (e.g., if you use this blender, you will be able to prepare dinner faster). For the past several decades, marketers and advertising practitioners have been banging the drum about focusing on benefits as the key to unlock consumers' wallets. However, benefits as they are presented today do not go nearly far enough. Perhaps we marketers have gotten lazy and have not pushed ourselves far enough in discovering new and creative benefits our products can provide. On the other hand, perhaps the product benefits can never go far enough, because benefits remain strongly left-brain oriented (e.g., saves time, saves money).

According to our research, people craft fantasies—sometimes very elaborate ones—about their purchases. They know what their purchases will feel like, what they will look like, how the acquisition of particular products will transform their lives and make them better, more successful, happier, more fulfilled people. That is what the anticipation cycle that precedes buying is all about. Fantasies about how the product will fill a missing aspect of one's life fire the imagination. This builds stress, "positive healthy stress," which is finally resolved in the act of purchase and initial excitement created by the acquisition. Then the cycle begins again, with new fantasies and new aspects of life that need satisfying.

SHOWTIME ROTISSERIE GRILL PRODUCT POSITIONING

FEATURES > Directly observable, physical characteristics

- Black and white
- Small size (demonstrated with toaster oven)
- Quality manufacturer (demonstrated with hammer hit)
- Cooks all kinds of meats (e.g., chicken, turkey, ribs, pork loin, rib roast, steaks, fish, lamb)
- Under $100 retail
- Comes complete with accessories, recipes, instructional video, heating disk

BENEFITS > Attributes that are the result of consumers using the product

- Saves electricity (uses 1200 watts just like a hair dryer)
- Saves time (less time to cook meats; 12 minutes per pound compared with 20 minutes in oven)
- Cooks entire dinner with warming tray for two side dishes
- Best-tasting meats, crispy on outside, juicy on inside
- Fat melts out of meats to make them healthier
- Best-tasting meat simply and easily
- Cooks premium meats like a professional
- Easy cleanup
- Long-lasting

VALUES > Personal values and beliefs that strongly motivate the consumer to buy

- "Hardworking people want to spend money on something that will last a lifetime." Grill becomes an essential part of your life conveying all its benefits (savings in energy; good, more healthful food; high quality; saved time) to the owner throughout his or her lifetime. Buy it and your life is instantly transformed.
- When you serve food from the grill, your guests will be amazed, give you 'applause' (as the audience applauds Ron); They will admire you, believing you cook as well as a professional. You will be a cooking "Hero."
- "This machine is my new husband." Ron's co-host makes this breathless statement, which is not explained, but presented for the audience to figure out. To me it implies that this machine grills better than my husband, helps me in the kitchen more than my husband, does work for me unlike my husband, gives unconditional support better than my husband. It's a weird statement, but it really underscores the message of life transformation through the appliance.
- Gives you a non-stress life. Easy cook-at-once meals without work; no need to be in the kitchen doing the hard work; you can be with guests. The grill does all the work for you. Audience member says, "So few products make your life more convenient." Several mentions are made of using the grill in RVs, suggesting that with this appliance you can achieve an RV-vacation lifestyle.

A brand or product platform describing the features, benefits, and life-transforming attributes gives marketers and advertisers the insights needed to touch customers' hot buttons with powerful and compelling marketing messages. Ronco knows how to play to consumer fantasies. As mentioned earlier, the 30-minute infomercial for the Ronco Showtime Grill provides a tutorial in how to position a mundane small appliance that cooks chicken, the most mundane of meats, as a means to transform your life from drab, dull, and ordinary into one that is more fulfilling, rewarding, and satisfying. By spending only $99, in five easy payments, you suddenly become a better person, a better homemaker and wife, admired by your friends and family, and more fulfilled in all aspects of your life.

SELLING TIP: *Sell the sizzle*

The prime motivator of desire is rooted in passion, not logic.

Eric Schulz, in his book, *The Marketing Game*, makes the assumption: "Consumers are logical. If you say something that makes sense, they will believe you." WRONG! This is wishful thinking on the part of consumer-product marketing executives. On the one hand, consumers are not logical, and what they want, desire, and dream of owning is not logical. On the other hand, they need logical reasons to justify the purchase of products they don't need. But the prime motivator of desire is rooted in passion, not logic. That is why consumer marketers need to come back again and again to selling the "sizzle," the wish fulfillment, the satisfaction of the consumer's fantasy.

I recently happened upon a Ralph Lauren commercial on television for its new Glamourous perfume. It shows actress Penelope Cruz and her date dressed in evening clothes walking in the rain to their car. As they dance and caress along the city streets, they are drenched in the rain, but clearly enjoying every minute of it. They are in public and formally dressed, but they act as if they are in the shower together getting ready for a night of steamy romance. The image is sexy and exciting, but I cannot escape the reality of this situation, which is a real turnoff, and get into the fantasy. Every rain shower that I have ever been in has given me a chill, even on the hottest summer day. Here is poor, underfed Penelope in a sleeveless evening gown walking completely unprotected in the pouring rain. Rain causes your makeup to run and your hair to become a mess, but Penelope's face is flawless and her hair, even soaking wet, looks great. Soaking wet clothes are literally a drag, but this couple is dancing around in the street. For me this ad pushes the sizzle envelope too far. A dark, dirty, smelly city street is not where I want to get caught in the rain in my evening clothes. In my fantasy, my date has an umbrella that he uses to sprint, alone, to the car, and he drives back for me.

Although the Glamourous ad failed to pull me in, water imagery is a recurring theme in advertising fantasy building. During focus groups where we studied consumers' motivations in buying things they don't need, participants were asked to clip ads and photographs from magazines that best exemplify products that transform their lives. They clipped pictures that talked deeply to them about their personal fantasies. Repeatedly, participants clipped images of water—bathtubs, whirlpools, pools, beaches, lakes—and most often these water images were linked with romance. They showed couples on a cruise ship, couples by the water, couples in a hot tub. In addition to being linked with romance, water imagery is also evocative of purity, cleanliness, nature and natural beauty, relaxation, and adventure. Bathrooms and kitchens figure prominently in consumers' life-transforming fantasies, supporting the link between kitchen appliances and life enhancement. Bedroom pictures in ads offer consumers' emotional succor. Outdoor scenes of lush backyards, mountains, valleys, and meadows promise a release from stress by returning to nature. You can sell the sizzle by presenting powerful emotional imagery that creates or extends a consumer's fantasy and the promise that the fantasy will be fulfilled by purchasing the featured product.

Brands that have life and vibrancy do so on an emotional plane.

SELLING TIP: *Fantasy branding can extend a franchise*

At its root, consumer product branding is all about sparking a consumer fantasy. Branding that goes only as far as brand features and benefits will be relegated to the waste dump of consumer brands. Brands that have life and vibrancy, that really speak to the customer, do so on an emotional plane. Coke, Disney, Chanel, Calvin Klein—all truly great brands—have harnessed the left-brain power of features and benefits with the transforming magic of right-brain emotion to craft an identity, personality, and value system that consumers can really accept.

Getting It Right

YANKEE CANDLE
Nobody holds a candle to Yankee

Holding the number-one position in the premium candle segment of the $2.4 billion retail market for candles, Yankee Candle benefited from "exploding growth in the candle category from 1994 to 1999, but that is only part of Yankee Candle's success story," explains Craig Rydin, President and CEO of Yankee Candle.

Since its founding over 30 years ago, Yankee Candle has been able to execute a brand-building strategy that resonates with the consumers. "Consumers today are getting more 'home-centric,' and what is more central to the home than the warmth and comfort a fragranced candle represents," Rydin says. "We have built the brand around the importance of fra-

grance in the home." Joining Yankee Candle this year after serving as President of Godiva Chocolatier, Rydin is no stranger to building a brand around "affordable indulgences that give the consumer a feeling of being special."

Along with the allure, romance, and emotional appeal that Yankee's core fragranced-candle products represent, the company has built a business on a commitment to strong financial fundamentals and business execution. "Yankee manages three core channels of distribution: captive retail, traditional wholesale distribution and consumer direct marketing through the internet and catalogs. This gives us key advantages so that Yankee outper-

Even in the realm of utilitarian purchases, there is opportunity for marketers to take their products to a new level. The Rubbermaid brand comes immediately to mind as one that understands how to communicate with its target market at an emotional level, as well as on a product features and benefits level. Rubbermaid means household organization. Like "Cleanliness is next to Godliness," an organized house is the ultimate achievement for homeowners, whether their realm is the garage and basement, or the kitchen, closets, bedrooms, bathrooms, and everywhere else. Since I am not blessed with the ability to organize my home or office or anything tangible, I am a complete sucker for anything that I can buy that will turn me into an "organized" person. Buckets, baskets, shelves, drawers, and all kinds

formed its competitive set in the very challenging macroeconomic environment it faced the fourth quarter of 2001," Rydin notes.

Key to building Yankee Candle's nationwide reputation as a premier candle brand is the company-owned chain of nearly 200 specialty retail stores. These stores, mostly mall based, are the "gold standard" for presenting the brand and the products to the consumer. "Our brand and its dominance is being driven by our captive-retail footprint," Rydin says. "Our strategy is not very different from many other national brands, like Godiva, that built an identity through multiple channels, especially captive retail."

The migration to company-owned-and-operated retail, while critical for the strength and continued growth of the brand, is a fairly recent development for the company. "Yankee Candle started in traditional wholesale distribution. Today we have some 13,000 stores that are our wholesale accounts," Rydin explains. "As we manage these two channels of distribution, the challenge is to present the same brand strategy in both places. We are moving toward a 'store-within-a-store' concept for our wholesale accounts. We want to present the essence of our brand consistently in our wholesale accounts as in our captive-retail stores. Communicating and building the brand is our priority."

The business of selling consumer indulgences has been good to Yankee Candle. Its business has nearly tripled since 1996, rising from $115 million to $339 million in 2000. Sales in the first nine months of 2001 are running 13 percent ahead of previous year, with significant growth tracked at the company's retail stores.

How will Yankee Candle continue its growth trajectory? "Home fragrance is what resonates with the consumer. Fragrance is the emotional bond that links Yankee Candle with our consumer and what brings them back again and again to our brand," Rydin says.

of organizers to hold things fill my house and office. The only problem for me is that once things are stored away, they are lost forever. So, I remain a disorganized, stack-them-in-a-pile type of person. However, I know in my heart that if I could only use all these wonderful Rubbermaid organizers and exercise organizational discipline, I would be transformed into a truly better, more fulfilled person who'd accomplish much more.

INDULGENCES ARE LIFE'S LITTLE LUXURIES BOUGHT WITHOUT GUILT

Offering high emotional gratification but being low on the extravagance scale, indulgences are described as "little" luxuries, something you can indulge in daily, without guilt or recrimination. One consumer, who collects, describes an indulgence this way: "Luxuries make me feel guilty. It's totally different to spend $25 to $50 on a 'Clark Gable' collector plate than to spend hundreds of dollars on a luxury. There is a difference in how much you spend." Another says, "An indulgence is something in excess of what you need, but not too much in excess." Unlike other discretionary purchases, which may demand more of a financial commitment, an indulgence is an everyday affair that involves spending only pocket change.

An indulgence pampers the individual. While it provides some physical satisfactions (e.g., features and benefits), its primary satisfaction is emotional. What kind of products constitute an indulgence? Here are some examples taken from our research:

- "An expensive bottle of wine is an indulgence."

- "For me, candles are my indulgence."

- "Bath salts from the Dead Sea."

- "I buy lots of books. I have a friend who thinks my books are a luxury. She says, 'that's what a library card is for.' But they are my books. There is a thrill in acquiring them. I don't read all of them, but I think someday I will have time and will be able to."

- "Every week my husband buys new DVDs. He likes to say he has them."

- "I just spent $400 on plants for my front porch and the fence. I love showing off my garden."

- "I bought a bottle of perfume for $75. I'm a woman, I have to smell good."

Items that exemplify the indulgence category include candles, higher-quality "lotions and potions," bath accessories, costume jewelry, collectibles, stuffed animals, toys and games, hobbies and crafts, sporting equipment, fresh flowers, gourmet foods, tabletop gifts, books, CDs, DVDs, and other entertainment products.

In the consumer's mind, indulgences, because they are not bought for functionality, always fall somewhere above utilitarian purchases, and below luxuries, which carry a heftier price tag. That's why we call indulgences "little" luxuries. They are those little purchases that give utmost gratification without guilt.

How much money people can spend without guilt varies from person to person and from item to item. For example, I feel guilty if I spend $300 on something for the home, such as a piece of furniture, a framed print (one of my weaknesses), or dinnerware (another weakness), because my husband views home-related purchases as decisions we should both make. On the other hand, I will spend $300 for a suit coat or blouse and skirt without thinking twice, not feeling guilty and never having to worry about spousal "approval." Yet I hesitate to spend $300 on a piece of jewelry, but it won't necessarily stop me if I have a "need" for it, such as buying a fabulous pin to accessorize the new $300 jacket I just bought. For another person, my $300 indulgence expenditure might be $30 or $3,000. The absolute dollar value is a function of income level and demographics, but that's not all. It is linked intimately to individual passion, value, and personal tastes for specific products. Because it is so highly individualized, consumer passion for indulgences needs to be carefully researched through psychographic analysis.

> **Psychographic studies survey motivations, drives, and passions.**

DISCOVER THE UNDERLYING PASSION THAT DRIVES INDULGENCE PURCHASES

Unlike demographic research, which focuses on quantifiable facts about consumers, such as income levels, marital status, household composition, age, and gender, psychographic studies survey motivations, drives, and passions. When you undertake a psychographic market study, you try to quantify and document the inner workings of the consumer's mind and heart. In effect, you turn the unspoken, unrealized, unconscious, imaginative, right-brain drive for a product into data that you can analyze with the business executive's left-brained mentality.

Sounds like so much hocus-pocus? Maybe, but psychographic market research helps uncover the interior emotional life of the consumer and can ultimately make sense of it so that marketing strategies can be devised, products competitively positioned, and advertising messages persuasively crafted. Psychographic studies often start with focus groups. Selected for these groups are consumers who have an interest in, or proven history of, buying a particular product. They are usually paid a fee for two hours of their time to sit around a table and talk about themselves and their desire for the product. A professional moderator keeps a focus group from descending into chaos and getting out of "focus." The moderator asks the right questions, probes further when a particular response suggests that more lies beneath the surface, and manages dichotomous voices who try to dominate the group or get off subject. These groups generate many pages of thorough, professionally written analysis of the major findings. We call them hypotheses theories to be tested in subsequent quantitative numbers-oriented research. Just as important are verbatim quotes from consumers about what does and doesn't excite them about the product in question.

Now comes the fun part where the hypotheses from the focus groups are tested and the dominating psychographic characteristics of the consumer target market are measured and quantified. Taking the exact same phrases and wording used by the consumers, the market researcher goes to the field with a questionnaire to which hundreds, even thousands of potential consumers can respond. A battery of attitudinal statements are presented to the target market asking them to what extent they agree or disagree with the statement. With a sufficient number of respondents (usually somewhere between 200 and 2,000), the results of the attitudinal questions can be grouped and classified according to the similarities or dissimilarities of responses. Using a cluster analysis program, market researchers can segment the target market into discreet groups or clusters based upon their attitudes, motivations, feelings, and emotions about the particular product. What is the right number of clusters? There is not a right or wrong number, but cognitive research has shown that the human mind is incapable of simultaneously maintaining a list of no more than nine individual items—thus our seven-digit telephone numbers. Moreover, if you are like me, you are seriously challenged with keeping a list of seven in mind at one time. In most psychographic studies I conduct, a four to five cluster solution is best. On a few occasions, I have found only a single cluster, which means that the target market is remarkably homogeneous in its attitude and feelings about the product. In others, I have gone to seven distinctly defined market segments.

Besides discovering the core motivations and emotions that drive different types of consumer to specific products, there are usually demographic differences among the clusters as well. These demographic differences provide marketers with measurable market segments to target through advertising-media selection.

CONSUMER MOTIVATION STUDY

To better understand why people buy things they don't need, Unity Marketing conducted a psychographic study of the typical American consumer. Using a battery of attitudinal statements centering on the emotional gratification of buying things they don't need, we asked respondents how much they agreed or disagreed with each statement. Using a cluster analysis program, five segments or clusters emerge when examining the attitudes and motivations that drive consumers to purchase these discretionary items:

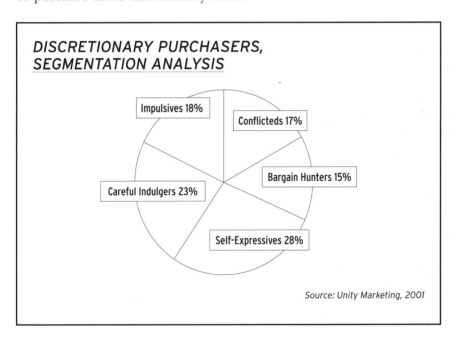

DISCRETIONARY PURCHASERS, SEGMENTATION ANALYSIS

Impulsives 18%
Conflicteds 17%
Bargain Hunters 15%
Careful Indulgers 23%
Self-Expressives 28%

Source: Unity Marketing, 2001

Now let's look more closely at the distinguishing characteristics.

SELF-EXPRESSIVES | CONSUMING AS A CREATIVE OUTLET

Self-Expressives use their consumption as a means of self-expression, reaffirming their personal identity to themselves and declaring it visually to others. Their purchases satisfy their desires and fantasies. They are highly involved in purchasing goods that enrich, enhance, or improve the quality of their lives. They tend to imbue the items they

A QUICK GUIDE TO THE SEGMENTS

Self-Expressives use their consumption as a means of self-expression, reaffirming their personal identity to themselves and declaring it symbolically to others. Their purchases satisfy their desires and fantasies. They are highly involved in purchasing goods that enrich, enhance, or improve the quality of their lives. Self-Expressives comprise the largest market segment, accounting for about 28 percent of all discretionary income consumers.

Careful Indulgers share many similarities with Self-Expressives, but exhibit a more practical, reasoned approach to their purchases of "Indulgences." They are less "driven" to make discretionary purchases and more "reasoned" in their purchases. Among all groups, these consumers rank two motivators highest: replacing an existing item and planned purchase. Unlike Self-Expressives, the Careful Indulgers gain less emotional satisfaction in making these purchases and are far less likely to make impulse purchases. Careful Indulgers are about 23 percent of all discretionary income consumers.

Impulsives buy discretionary purchases to indulge themselves on the spur of the moment. They purchase these products for the sheer joy and pleasure the purchases bring. Their thrill is in buying products that they desire. Unlike Self-Expressives and Careful Indulgers, Impulsives are not motivated by the need to express themselves, their personalities, and value systems, in the purchases they make. For them, consuming and buying is the end in itself. Impulsives represent about 18 percent of discretionary income consumers.

Conflicteds, just as their segment name implies, feel conflicted about satisfying their desire for discretionary products. They don't see their consumer behavior as an expressive outlet, yet they desire to buy these products. However, they have mixed feelings about making such "unnecessary" purchases and so tend to feel guilty after buying or have a feeling of letdown once they make a purchase. They don't obtain the same level of pleasure or emotional enjoyment from their consumption that other segments do. Conflicteds comprise about 17 percent of the total market.

Bargain Hunters are the least highly involved consumers of discretionary items. Compared with all the other segments, they derive the least amount of pleasure and emotional gratification from buying. They are also the least likely of all segments to make an impulse purchase, and they are the least likely to be motivated by desire to improve the quality of life. They look for bargains when they shop and tend to carefully evaluate the pluses and minuses before making a purchase decision. Bargain-hunters comprise the smallest market segment, only about 15 percent of the market.

buy with special meaning and may even look at some favorite items like "members of the family."

The Self-Expressive type of consumer uses shopping and personal consumption as a creative outlet. The act of consuming is highly emotional. Self-Expressives look to their discretionary purchases to satisfy their emotional needs.

Because they seek to express themselves through their consumption and the purchases they make, they are highly idiosyncratic in their purchases. That is, what turns on one self-expressive individual may be very different from what turns on another. However, some common threads emerge in the purchase patterns of these highly individualistic consumers.

They are driven by a desire to "fit in" with their aspirational group. While they are individualistic, they don't want to venture too far afield from their peer group. For example, Self-Expressives will strictly avoid painting their houses the same shade of blue as their neighbor's, yet certainly won't paint their homes a deep purple or shocking pink. Rather, they will seek to find a special shade of blue that allows them to express their individuality within the context of what is "acceptable," but not exactly like everybody else's.

With their strong emotional drive to consume, Self-Expressives respond sentimentally to items with a nostalgia appeal that takes them back to a "golden age," usually back to their youth. Any number of social trends point to this drive for nostalgia, including the collecting boom in toys, dolls, and games from the 1950s and 1960s; the explosion of online auctions, typified by eBay; and the PT Cruiser from Chrysler. Seeking out a "golden age" is a major motivator for Self-Expressives and a key to understanding their form of consumption as an outlet for personal identity and self-expression.

Demographic characteristics of self-expressive consumers

This is the largest market segment. It is composed of equal shares of baby boomers, the generation born between 1946 and 1964, (38 percent), and GenXers and their younger counterparts, (38 percent), all born in 1965 or later. About one-fourth of the segment was born before 1946, making them members of the World War II and the Swing generations.

While just over half of Self-Expressives are married, one-fourth are single, never married, and 10 percent are divorced.

DIFFERING ATTITUDES AMONG SEGMENTS

	Bargain-Hunter	Self-Expressive	Careful Indulger	Impulsive	Conflicted
You get a feeling of personal satisfaction when you make a discretionary purchase	Disagree	Strongly Agree	Agree	Agree	Agree
Before you make a discretionary purchase, you spend time anticipating the purchase, evaluating the pros and cons	Agree	Agree	Agree	Disagree	Agree
You often make a discretionary purchase on the spur of the moment	Disagree	Agree	Disagree	Agree	Agree
You make discretionary purchases because they will make your life more pleasant and satisfying	Disagree	Strongly Agree	Agree	Agree	Agree
You get a thrill out of buying something special that you don't need but desire	Disagree	Agree	Disagree	Agree	Neutral
You feel guilty after you make a discretionary purchase	Disagree	Disagree	Disagree	Disagree	Neutral
After you make a discretionary purchase, you feel a letdown when you get it home	Disagree	Disagree	Disagree	Disagree	Disagree
You express different sides of your personality with the discretionary purchases that you make	Disagree	Strongly Agree	Agree	Agree	Agree
The discretionary items that you purchase set you apart from your neighbors and friends and make you unique	Strongly Disagree	Strongly Agree	Disagree	Disagree	Disagree

Women are more highly represented than men in this segment.

Compared with the other segments, the Self-Expressives are more ethnically diverse.

All income levels are represented in this segment, although only about 37 percent of Self-Expressives report an income of $50,000 or more. While this consumer segment is not the most affluent, the consumers in this segment spend the highest percentage of their income on discretionary purchases (19.5 percent).

Self-Expressives agree most strongly with these statements:

- "You get a feeling of personal satisfaction when you make a discretionary purchase for yourself or your household."

DIFFERING ATTITUDES *(Continued)*

	Bargain-Hunter	Self-Expressive	Careful Indulger	Impulsive	Conflicted
It is more satisfying when you have to search to find a discretionary item that is very special to buy	Disagree	Strongly Agree	Agree	Neutral	Disagree
The discretionary items you buy for yourself and your home make your life more meaningful	Strongly Disagree	Agree	Agree	Neutral	Neutral
The discretionary items that you buy help you fulfill your longings	Strongly Disagree	Strongly Agree	Neutral	Neutral	Disagree
You often purchase a discretionary item because it has a symbolic meaning or links with memories of the past	Disagree	Agree	Disagree	Disagree	Neutral
You seek instant gratification through discretionary purchases	Disagree	Agree	Disagree	Agree	Disagree
You look for bargains and sales when purchasing discretionary items	Agree	Agree	Agree	Agree	Agree
You spend more money on discretionary items today than you did in the early 1990s	Disagree	Strongly Agree	Agree	Agree	Disagree
Your family, coworkers, and friends influence you in making discretionary purchases	Disagree	Neutral	Disagree	Disagree	Neutral

- "You make discretionary purchases because they will make your life more pleasant and satisfying."

- "You express different sides of your personality with the discretionary purchases that you make."

- "The discretionary items that you purchase set you apart from your neighbors and friends and make you unique." Boomers and older consumers don't agree, while GenXers and younger Self-Expressives do.

- "It is more satisfying when you have to search to find a discretionary item that is very special to buy."

- "The discretionary items you buy for yourself and your home make your life more meaningful."

- "The discretionary items you buy help you fulfill your longings."

- "You spend more money on discretionary items today than you did in the early 1990s."

MOST ACTIVE BUYERS

TREND WATCH: These Self-Expressive consumers will continue to be the most active buying segment in the future. They deprive themselves of nothing, and while the potential impact of an economic downturn cannot be anticipated, these consumers give signs of not letting something as "insignificant" as not having money keep them from pursuing their consuming passions. Consumer product companies should target this segment by aligning their products with these youthful, self-expressive, and self-indulgent consumers.

CAREFUL INDULGERS | THOUGHTFUL PLEASURE-BUYING

Careful Indulgers share many similarities with Self-Expressives, but exhibit a more practical and reasoned approach to their purchases of "Indulgences." They are less "driven" to make discretionary purchases and more "reasoned" in their purchases. These consumers are more likely make discretionary purchases due to rational motivators, such as to replace a worn-out item or to make a planned purchase. Unlike Self-Expressives, Careful Indulgers gain less emotional satisfaction in making these purchases and are far less likely to make impulse purchases.

They tend to see themselves as similar to their peers and, unlike the Self-Expressives, do not feel the need to declare their identity through their consumption. They are unlikely to ascribe special meaning to the items they buy or to animate them in their imaginations.

They enjoy the "hunt" to find a desirable item. They are not inclined toward making spur-of-the-moment decisions and impulsive purchases. If they find something they want, they are likely to go home and think about it and discuss it with their significant others before making the purchase.

Items, things, consumables do not hold the same meaning for Careful Indulgers that they do to the Self-Expressives. They look upon things as things, not symbolic representations of their personality and value system.

Demographic characteristics of careful indulgers

Careful Indulgers are more likely to be baby boomers and have moderate household incomes under $50,000. They are more likely to be married than Self-Expressives. Women are also slightly more represented among Careful Indulgers (53 percent) than men (47 percent).

Careful Indulgers are more likely than any other segment to live in two-person households and less likely to have children living in the home.

They spend, on average, about 13.4 percent of income on "Indulgent" purchases.

While people in this segment are more reasoned in their approach to "Indulgence" purchases, they are fairly active buyers in most categories. They tend to look at their purchases from a more practical orientation, but are hesitant to deny themselves these indulgences.

IMPULSIVES | SEE IT; LIKE IT; BUY IT

Impulsives buy indulgent discretionary purchases on the spur of the moment. They purchase these products for the sheer joy and pleasure the purchase brings. Their thrill is in buying products that they desire. Unlike Self-Expressives, Impulsives are not particularly motivated by the need to express themselves, their personalities, and their value systems in the purchases they make. For them, consuming and buying is the end in itself.

As big spenders and active purchasers in the discretionary product categories, these consumers differ from the Self-Expressives mainly because they don't ascribe a higher meaning or value in their consuming behavior. Things do not become symbols of one's identity. In fact, once these indulgent consumers get their purchases home, they are likely to be lost or forgotten. These consumers are very active buyers, but driven to purchase by what strikes their fancy at the moment, not like Self-Expressives who look for more "meaning" in their purchases. While the Self-Expressives will treasure their things, the

Impulsives are driven much more by the need to acquire and keep acquiring new things.

Demographic characteristics of impulsives

Impulsives are represented equally by boomers and GenXers, at 41 percent for each group. While represented among all income levels, the Impulsives are most likely to have incomes in the $35,000–to–$49,999 range.

Men are slightly more likely to be an Impulsive type of consumer. Compared with the other consumer segments, Impulsives are more likely to be single, never married.

Impulsives, along with Self-Expressives, spend the highest percentage of household income on discretionary products (19.3 percent).

Impulsives agree most strongly with these statements:

- "You often make a discretionary purchase on the spur of the moment."

- "You spend more money on discretionary items today than you did in the early 1990s."

CONFLICTEDS | SHOULD I, SHOULDN'T I?

These consumers feel conflicted about satisfying their desire for products they don't need. They don't see their consumer behavior as an expressive outlet, yet they desire to buy these products. However, they have mixed feelings about making such "unnecessary" purchases and so they may tend to feel guilty after buying. They do not obtain the same level of pleasure or emotional satisfaction from their consumption that other segments do, largely because they suffer so much internal conflict before the purchase.

For Conflicteds, the educational aspect of their discretionary purchases is of prime importance, so they are more likely to buy computers, books, and other educationally oriented products. Perhaps owing in some small part to their feeling of conflict in their consuming behavior, they highly value stress relief and relaxation in the discretionary purchases they make.

Demographic characteristics of conflicteds

Conflicteds are more likely than any other segment to have a house-hold income under $35,000. Nearly half (46 percent) of Conflicteds are boomers. They spend about 12.7 percent of income on discretionary purchases.

This is the segment with the highest incidence of women and divorced or separated individuals. Forty-six percent have children in the home, the highest of any group. With this incidence of children, it is easy to see where the "conflict" in making indulgent purchases comes from.

BARGAIN-HUNTERS | IS IT ON SALE?

If Self-Expressives are the most highly involved consumers of discretionary items, Bargain-Hunters are the least. Compared with all other segments, they derive the least amount of pleasure and emotional gratification from buying. They are also the least likely of all segments to make an impulse purchase. Of all segments, they are the least motivated by the desire to improve the quality of life. They look for bargains when they shop and tend to evaluate carefully the pluses and minuses before making a purchase decision. Buying things they do not need just doesn't turn them on.

Demographic characteristics of bargain-hunters

Men dominate this segment, with women representing only 41 percent of the total segment.

Compared with other segments, Bargain Hunters have a higher incidence of WWII and Swing generation consumers (35 percent). They are *not* the lowest income segment. Rather, the highest distribution in this segment falls in the $50,000-to-$74,999 income range. Given their older demographics, they are the segment least likely to have children in the home. They spend the lowest percentage of income on discretionary purchases (10.5 percent).

WITH INDULGENCES, MORE IS BETTER!

It is probably more than coincidence that the United States is both the world's wealthiest country and the fattest. This country is headed for a public health crisis of direst proportions with nearly 40 million

Americans certifiably obese. The nation's obesity rate stood at 19.8 percent in 2000, up from a 12 percent rate or "less than ten years before," in 1991. Obesity, defined as a body-mass index of 30 or more, is linked to diabetes. Further, obesity-related diseases are second only to smoking as the leading cause of premature deaths. Today more than one-half of Americans (56.4 percent) are overweight (body-mass index of at least 25), compared with 45 percent in 1991. That leaves a "slim" minority of Americans with a healthy weight, who eat a moderate diet, and get adequate exercise.

In some consumer circles, immoderation in spending is linked to immoderation in eating. After all, the same emotional needs drive many consumers to both spend too much and eat too much. There is a reason that gluttony is one of the seven deadly sins, and some American consumers are as guilty of voracious shopping as they are of gluttonous eating.

There already is enough literature available about American consumers' propensity to over-spend. John De Graaf's *Affluenza: The All-Consuming Epidemic*, presented as a PBS special along with a published companion book, is one of the best and most damning. **A warning:** As marketers, we who want to capture a greater share of consumer spending, even over-spending, need to be aware of the negative side of emotional spending and how some consumers gluttonously shop and buy.

As a "consumer in training" under the tutelage of my mother, I learned that it was better to spend money on one very good-quality item that would last than to spend the same amount on many items of lesser quality. Thus, I have a propensity to buy classic-tailored clothes in neutral colors that I can wear for at least several seasons. However, when consumers buy indulgences, those early lessons about putting quality above quantity just don't apply. Since people buy indulgences primarily for immediate emotional gratification, fineness and high quality are not an essential issue. An indulgence isn't to be enjoyed for long or forever. Its satisfactions are transitory. Indulgences need only provide satisfaction for the moment.

Because indulgences are for the here and now, the more you buy, the better, or so the thinking goes among some consumers. That is one reason why "buy two, get one free" and "buy one get the next for half-price" offers are so incredibly compelling for indulgence-type items. Because indulgences are often spur-of-the-moment purchases, a dynamite sale or special offer is overwhelmingly compelling to get consumers to open their wallets and buy. One focus group respondent explains it this way: "I buy clothes all the time and shoes. I love shoes and buy shoes I don't need. I am in Payless twice a week buying shoes I don't need. I spend $30 a month on shoes. I can buy more shoes at Payless than anywhere. If I see a sale, buy one get one half off, I HAVE to go in. I'm a real bargain shopper."

The cosmetic companies have learned the drawing power of sampling as a marketing strategy that gives more to the consumer. Twice a year cosmetic companies package their samples into gift cases and make a big deal out of their gift-with-purchase sales. How many of these cosmetic companies' regular, dedicated shoppers hold off buying until the gift-with-purchase sale? The shoppers don't need the gifts that are offered. Many times they don't even use the colors and products included. But that special free gift makes them feel like a "winner." They got something extra. They got more than they paid for. That is marketing magic and a promotional strategy that should be borrowed by many indulgence product marketers.

In other words, in marketing indulgence-type products, quality takes a back seat to quantity, given the fleeting nature of emotional enjoyment. Further, for many of these products, such as flowers, candles, bath-and-body lotions and potions, greeting cards, and collectibles, it may be hard to discern differences in quality between one product and another. That may be why some marketers that have attempted to move certain indulgence products up-market to the luxury realm have been less than successful in their attempts. For example, in today's market, while there are premium brands, no brand of true luxury candles exists. Perhaps because of the consumable nature of the product and consumers' inability to distinguish quality differences between one brand and another, there never will be.

LIFESTYLE AND ASPIRATIONAL LUXURIES LET YOU LIVE THE LIFE OF THE "RICH & FAMOUS"

We define the third and fourth sectors in the discretionary product matrix as Lifestyle Luxuries and Aspirational Luxuries. Lifestyle luxuries are those luxury goods, which while they are considered a luxury, also offer a practical usefulness or utility for the consumer. Luxury cars, watches, china, furniture, and designer clothes are all lifestyle luxuries that serve a practical purpose. By comparison, aspirational luxuries, rather than providing some practical use, give primarily emotional satisfaction. Aspirational luxuries include such purchases as original art, antiques and vintage collectibles, boats and yachts, and fine jewelry. But whether the consumer is purchasing a lifestyle or aspirational luxury product, the drives and motivations are the same: they are looking for the "ultimate" in the luxury product that they buy.

So what does "luxury good" really mean? The *New Oxford American Dictionary* defines luxury as, "The state of great comfort and extravagant living; an inessential, desirable item that is expensive or difficult to obtain." A focus group respondent explained it this way: "A luxury is more than extra. It's more, more." The word luxury comes from the Latin "luxuria" which means "excess." Charles J. Reid, research associate in law and history at Emory University, defines luxury goods: "The operational definition of a luxury good is a good 95 percent of which is accessible to only 5 percent of the population." Jeremy Sampson, managing director of Interbrand Sampson, sees a luxury this way: "To some, it's an object of desire, sometimes aspirational, sometimes almost lust. I t will be financially expensive, perhaps self-indulgent and certainly not indispensable. It says: 'I've done it,' but that's crass. Sometimes it's a physical statement, as with a luxury car or an exquisite watch, pen, or piece of jewelery. Or as the Richemont annual report defines it: 'A luxury product is both an object and a catalyst for thought ... the aim of a luxury brand is to awaken desire and pleasure.'"

While what is defined as a luxury good is fluid over time and may differ depending on the socio-economic level, the best definition of a luxury good in contemporary America is "Brand" and its positioning as the "best of the best." The brand identifies the product as a luxury.

Luxuries are brands

Women's Wear Daily recently reported its fifth annual consumer survey of luxury fashion brands. The survey measured consumers' familiarity with the brand, their perception of the brand as a "luxury" brand, their purchase incidence, and what luxury fashion brand they would buy if money were no object. The top five luxury fashion brands according to *Women's Wear Daily* are Rolex, Tiffany, Cartier, Versace, and Giorgio Armani. Lifestyle luxuries, those luxuries that offer some functional, practical use are almost always linked with a brand. In effect, the brand acts like the "Good Housekeeping Seal of

LUXURY BRANDS

2001 sales (U.S.$ millions) and percent change 2000-2001

Brand	Sales 2001	Percent change 2000-2001
Pinault-Printemps-Redoute	$23,308.0	22.4%
Christian Dior **	11,174.0	26.7
LVMH **	10,909.0	27.0
Richemont	3,237.5	15.9
Swatch **	2,563.3	12.5
Gucci	2,258.5	8.7
Polo Ralph Lauren	1,982.4	1.7
Tommy Hilfiger	1,880.9	4.9
Tiffany & Co.	1,658.1	14.1
Hermes *	1,090.9	16.8
Waterford Wedgewood **	1,021.3	15.1
Armani **	972.6	11.6
Donna Karan **	662.7	0.1
Bulgari **	636.6	17.9
Coach	616.1	12.2
IT Holdings/Ittierre **	432.9	12.9
Versace **	425.5	1.5
Movado	320.8	8.7
Average	$3,511.3	16.9%

Private: Estimates Hoovers Online
**FY 2000 reporting; percent change 1999-2000*

Approval" telling us that this functionally practical product is elevated above its more ordinary competitors. A luxury Rolex watch tells time, as does a Timex, but it does it with much more style and cachet. The brand, Rolex, is the pedigree saying this watch—this brand—is better than all the rest.

Looking beyond the fashion arena, there are luxury brands in many different categories of discretionary purchases, although fashion is one of the fields where luxury brands predominate. In the decade of the 1990s, investing in luxury brands was good business, as consumers yearned for these visible status symbols that proclaimed their wealth, status, and good taste. From 2000 to 2001, the leading luxury brands averaged a growth rate reaching 17 percent, dynamic growth for any product category. After the 9/11 terrorist attack, luxury brand growth is settling down to more normal levels, as consumers shy away from purchases that are perceived as "too extravagant" in the new economy. But what is perceived as "too extravagant" varies from consumer to consumer, so we may well find the typical Rolex shopper trading down to a Movado, or the Louis Vuitton handbag buyer stepping back to Coach. They still are shopping in the luxury arena; they are just pulling back from the more extravagant examples.

While luxury brands face new marketing challenges in the aftermath of 9/11, these brands are extremely hard to "kill off." Why? Because they have taken so many years to foster and build. Few luxury brands are created overnight. Rather, many brands go back more than a hundred years, like Cartier, founded in 1847, Tiffany dating from 1837, Rolex from 1908, Gucci from 1923. The closest we come to "instant" luxury brands is in the fashion arena. Contemporary designers, such as Donna Karan, Ralph Lauren, and Tommy Hilfiger to name a few, have crafted a luxury image through highly exclusive distribution, couture prices, fashion-forward but not jarring designs, and carefully selected licensing partnerships.

Licensing and its role in propagating a brand image is one of those business secrets most companies would rather keep hidden from their consuming public. Licensing is a legal agreement that allows one company to "borrow" the brand name, its logos, its image, its reputation, and put it on the borrowing company's products. Owners of luxury brands must walk a tight line between extending their brand too far into too many product categories and controlling it so tightly that revenue and brand-building potential are too restricted. On the surface, licensing looks like an easy way to cash in on the value of the brand without risking anything. After all, the licensor picks up the tab and pays royalties and minimums to boot.

But over the years, companies such as Christian Dior and Oscar de la Renta have discovered the hazards of extending their brands too far. Consequently, they responded by cutting way back on their licenses. Free use of licensing inevitably cheapens the brand and threatens its exclusivity. That is why Calvin Klein recently fought its jean's licensee, Warnaco, so hard. Calvin Klein claimed Warnaco violated its licensing agreement by distributing the Calvin Klein jeans through discount outlets. For a luxury brand, that will never do! Yet, luxury brands are remarkably resilient. They do not die easily, especially those enduring brands whose identity has been crafted over many decades, even centuries. Thus, previously over-licensed brands such as Christian Dior can pick themselves up, dust themselves off, and continue moving on in the luxury arena, even after a brief foray into the mass market. On the other hand, the more instant luxury brands, such as contemporary fashion brands, are more vulnerable to losing their cachet, since they haven't forged a solid reputation based upon many years of diligent brand management.

Consumers choose their luxuries

One of the common definitions of luxury goods is products and services that only the top 5 percent of U.S. households can afford. However, the luxury business has not chalked up double-digit growth throughout the past decade by selling only to the ultra-rich. After all, the numbers speak for themselves. There are a lot more moderately affluent Americans than super-rich ones. With household incomes of $145,000 and above, the top 5 percent of U.S. households by income number only 5.3 million, while 42.6 million households boast mid-to-upper incomes of $50,000 or more.

A new egalitarianism has taken over in today's luxury market. In America, luxury products can be bought by anyone up and down the economic ladder. While the nation's ultra-rich may well limit all their personal consumption to luxury brands, the real growth in the luxury market has come from the middle and upper-middle classes reaching up to buy luxury goods. Recognizing that everyone wants a piece of the "good life," luxury marketers have started to expand their product lines by offering small novelties and lower-priced goods that carry the brand name. Like Mercedes-Benz, which introduced its new C-Class of "affordable" luxury cars, other luxury marketers have been working on strategies to move down the price-point scale. The challenge is how to keep the exclusivity and brand image at the upper tier, while offering lower-priced models that appeal to and can be afforded by the less than "ultra-rich." Early evidence is that luxury marketers have had success moving downscale to capture market share from the mid-to-upper-income consumers, while maintaining the exclusive brand cachet that results from selling to the rich.

Along with a new egalitarianism in luxury goods comes consumers' ability to choose their luxuries. Today, consumers, armed with more information than ever before, can pick the aspects of their lives they wish to luxuriate, by buying luxury brands selectively. For everything else, there is the ordinary, everyday, and commonplace. For example, one consumer may buy only the top, luxury-cookware brands for her kitchen, while buying more everyday brands for bed or bath. Another might express his enthusiasm for a wine-tasting hobby by buying luxury brands of wine, wine glasses, and everything else that is involved with wine tasting, while sticking to more mundane brands in kitchen appliances, bedding, and clothes.

Consumers use brands as a way to sift out the trash from the treasure.

Faith Popcorn in her book, *EVEolution*, makes the point that women don't buy brands— they "join them." I believe this applies equally to men. In fact, the way the typical consumer thinks about and interacts with brands has undergone a sea change in the past twenty years. Inundated with hundreds of thousands of new products each year and endless media advertisements, consumers use brands as a way to sift out the trash from the treasure. A consumer is much more likely to notice a commercial message linked to a brand that the consumer has experienced before than one not so advantaged. We saw a real-life example of the concept of the consumers' belonging to a brand when Coca-Cola tried to introduce its New-Coke formula. Consumers were outraged that the company would dare to interfere with their favorite product. The marketplace spoke: "Coke belongs to us! You may be the company that makes it, but Coke is OURS, so don't mess with it." The passing of the Oldsmobile brand resulted in no such consumer outcry. That brand had lost its market and its connection with consumers.

More than other everyday brands, luxury brands evoke a strong and lasting image in the consumer's heart and mind. Consumers buy these brands to belong to them, to make the brand a part of themselves and their identities. For the most-involved consumers, the brand confers status on the owner, but it's more than that. It becomes part of these consumers' personal identities, who they are, and what their value systems are. The passionate way consumers interact with their favorite brands is almost spiritual in nature. It goes beyond logic and reason to the depths of one's personal identity.

This high level of involvement draws certain consumers, but it may well repel others, as it did for the respondent who strenuously objected to linking her name and identity with the Mercedes brand. "To me, luxury is all about your value system. It's about your beliefs, your religious system, your personality. I don't need a Mercedes. [Owning a Mercedes] is not an example we want to set. Even if I got a great deal on a Mercedes, I would not buy that. I don't need that kind of luxury. That brand is not me. I don't have that lifestyle." This consumer was adamant and highly emotional about NOT wanting to be linked to Mercedes and what that brand stands for. Even if she found a bargain on a used Mercedes, she would *never* buy that car because the brand repels her.

Luxury is to see and be seen

In marketing luxury products, there is clearly an aspirational component at play. Logo marks on many luxury goods are standard. Through them, the owner proclaims to the world his or her good taste and sophistication. Some consumers belong to a brand and they want the world to know about it. Fashion, cars, handbags and briefcases, jewelry, and watches are all luxury goods where brand logos are displayed. On the other hand, many classes of luxury goods are used privately and not exposed to public scrutiny. For these purchases, such as home furnishings, major appliances, and bedding, the consumer is driven to the luxury brand for personal motivations, not to see and be seen.

Juliet Schor, senior lecturer and director of women's studies at Harvard University, has published a number of books that focus on the aspirational nature of consumption. To Schor, consuming is a competitive sport that people participate in with their co-workers, family, neighbors, and friends. My research sees the primary driver for discretionary spending as the inner life of consumers and their needs and desires. In contrast, Schor's research on cosmetic consumption illustrates that for certain people under certain circumstances, the need to see and be seen is important in their choice of luxury brands.

In *The Overspent American*, Schor gives a nod to the role of emotional gratification in cosmetic purchases: "But despite its dubious effectiveness [e.g., cosmetics that promise clinical effects], women keep on buying the stuff. They shell out hundreds, even thousands, for wrinkle cream, moisturizers, eye shadows and powders, lip-

Consumers buy to make the brand a part of their identities.

sticks, and facial makeup. And why? One explanation is that they are looking for affordable luxury, the thrill of buying at the expensive department store, indulging in a fantasy of beauty and sexiness, buying 'hope in a bottle.' Cosmetics are an escape from an otherwise all-too-drab everyday existence. To Schor however, the primary driver is status, "Even in cosmetics—which is hardly the first product line that

Getting It Right

BULGARI

Its name is synonymous with "Luxury"

Bulgari used to be a brand known only to the rich and famous, but today it is expanding its horizons and opening its doors to well-heeled customers worldwide. Bulgari Chief Executive,

Francesco Trapani has moved to diversify the company's offerings beyond its core business of jewelry and watches to a range of other luxury products and services. "Today, Bulgari has a diversified product portfolio that foresees jewels and watches as the core business of the company, but that also includes perfume, scarves, ties, eyewear, and home designs. Bulgari is a luxury brand that offers products with a very distinctive style, at high prices, of outstanding quality," Trapani says.

As the company expands its realm into other luxury goods, it remains firmly grounded in the jewelry business. "Bulgari is a diversified jeweler, meaning that our core business is jewels and watches among other luxury products, but we will always remain a jeweler. We are 'The Italian Contemporary Jewellers,'" Trapani explains. Founded by Sotirio Bulgari in 1879, Bulgari's shop in via dei Condotti was renovated in 1932 when sons Giorgio and Constantino Bulgari inherited the business. Today that same shop serves as Bulgari's flagship store.

International expansion began during the 1970s when Bulgari stores were opened in New York, Geneva, Monte Carlo, and Paris. Today Bulgari's empire extends to more than 150 stores worldwide, including those in London, Milan, Munich, and St. Moritz as well as Hong Kong, Singapore, Osaka, and Tokyo. In 2001, net revenues grew 13 percent, from Euro 676 million in 2000 to Euro 766 million. Geographically, 14 percent of revenues are generated in Italy, with 26 percent coming from other European markets. Japan captures 22 percent of company revenues, while other Far Eastern markets comprise 17 percent. In 2001 the Americas produced 15 percent of total revenues, but it was the only market where Bulgari's sales declined over the previous year, down 17 percent to Euro 188 million. Trapani explains, "This is a difficult moment, not only because of September 11th, but during the summer of 2001 business was starting to slow down, because of a general economic downturn especially in the United States."

Tracking along with international expansion is Bulgari's broadening luxury product offerings. Trapani explains the diversification strategy, "Today, one can walk into a Bulgari store and buy a tie, a pair of sunglasses, or a perfume—products that cost much less than a jewel. Furthermore, there are some products within our core business, such as the B.zero1 jewelry collection or the Solotempo watch, that are entry-price products. It allows us to have a Bulgari product at an accessible price. We aim to reach all those who look for luxury products with a distinctive design of outstanding quality." In 2001, 38 percent of net revenues were derived from jewelry, with watches, 39 percent; perfumes, 16 percent; and accessories, 5 percent, comprising the bulk of sales. The company also generates about 2 percent of sales in licensing royalties and revenues from agreements with Luxottica for eyeware and Rosenthal, part of Waterford Wedgwood PLC, in Home Designs.

Looking toward the future, the company foresees major opportunities from its Bulgari Hotels & Resorts joint venture with Marriott International's new Luxury Group. The plan is to open seven exclusive Bulgari five-star hotels, most of them located in big cities but also including one or two resorts. This is a category slated for significant growth as the hotels and resorts offer their clientele an opportunity to vicariously experience the Bulgari lifestyle. Trapani envisions the hotels as a key foundation

for Bulgari's overall brand strategy. "The return on investment makes it a very interesting deal. While we are attracted to this joint venture for its significant investment potential, we also see huge cross-marketing possibilities between the Bulgari stores and the hotels. The client base of the stores is very similar to the hotels. For example, I think it is reasonable to assume that a couple would buy the engagement ring at Bulgari's, do the wedding party at a Bulgari hotel, and go to our resort during their honeymoon. Furthermore, we see those seven hotels as seven public relations "machines" for the Bulgari brand. These hotels will become a reference point for the local community, meaning that the café and restaurant will also attract the local crowd."

On the future of luxury brands, Trapani anticipates changes on the horizon. "Given the present business landscape, I foresee that only the strongest, most solid brands in the luxury business, like Bulgari, will survive. We will probably see many of the smaller brands disappear. People, though, will always be interested in luxury products."

comes to mind as a status symbol—there's a structure of one-up-womanship."

Schor explores the status component in cosmetics by looking at brand purchasing patterns for four different cosmetic products: lipsticks, eye shadows, mascara, and facial cleansers. What distinguishes each product is its relative visibility to others. For example facial cleansers are the least socially visible product since consumers use them in private, whereas lipstick is the most visible since it is accepted to touch up one's lipstick at the table and in public. Her research findings: women are far more likely to buy expensive lipsticks than they are to buy expensive facial cleansers. Her research leads her to conclude that consumers buy top-end brands of visible products far more than high-quality invisible ones.

To see and be seen plays a role in the purchase of luxury products. How important it really is for each brand, each product, is highly individualistic to each consumer, but marketers are strongly advised to study the role that visibility plays in the purchasing behavior of their consumer markets. For the ultra-high-end fashion brands, the obvious display of a brand logo is considered gauche and "nouveau riche." For other brands, a visible label clearly conveys value to the consumer. How much inherent value does the Mercedes-Benz hood ornament carry in the total cost of the car? What is a Chanel bag worth without the CC? How much does the polo symbol add to the value of a Ralph Lauren oxford shirt?

Luxury is in the eye of the beholder

In the final analysis, the consumer defines luxury. For one consumer, at one income level, with a passion for some aspect of his or her life—fashion, gourmet cooking, wine tasting, entertaining, home decorating—a particular item, brand, or product might be considered a luxury that is prized. For another, the same thing might be a total waste, or it may not be luxurious enough. Luxury products and brands, just like all discretionary expenditures, exist on a sliding scale that is measured in the perceptions, values, and experiences of the individual consumer. Increasingly luxury marketers are testing how far their brands can extend both up and down this consumer-defined sliding scale of values. While luxury brands must exercise great caution at the low and mid ranges of any product category, there is ample room to move along from upper-end to extravagant to luxury products, without necessarily losing brand perception and exclusivity.

Chapter 4

JUSTIFIERS GIVE CONSUMERS PERMISSION TO BUY

Consumers need a reason to buy things they don't need. For products deemed necessities, like milk, coffee, bread, and meat, the need itself provides permission. For things consumers don't need, i.e., discretionary purchases, they give themselves "permission" to buy by stacking various rationally based justifiers in favor of the purchase. It is the justifiers that give consumers the illusion that they are acting rationally in purchasing, but in reality, they remain driven by personal desires and emotions.

The perceived extravagance of a particular purchase usually determines how many justifiers are needed and to what extent. For example, a householder who wants to replace a 15-year-old sofa that is musty smelling and stained needs fewer justifiers than does one who wants to replace a 2-year-old sofa.

In the battle for consumers' wallets, marketers need to understand how to engage them on an emotional level. They need to give customers sufficient justifiers to overcome purchase barriers. The best salespeople understand how to overcome objections to reach a sale. Unfortunately, many marketers have distanced themselves too far from the sales process. They have forgotten, or don't understand, the critical role that overcoming objections plays in the sales process.

Salespeople overcome objections interactively and in real time. Marketers must do it indirectly through marketing communications, advertisements, point-of-purchase, and the purchase offer. They must anticipate the range of objections customers may present to keep from buying. Justifiers are the tools that marketers use to overcome objections in the store, at the mall, at the point of sale. When marketers

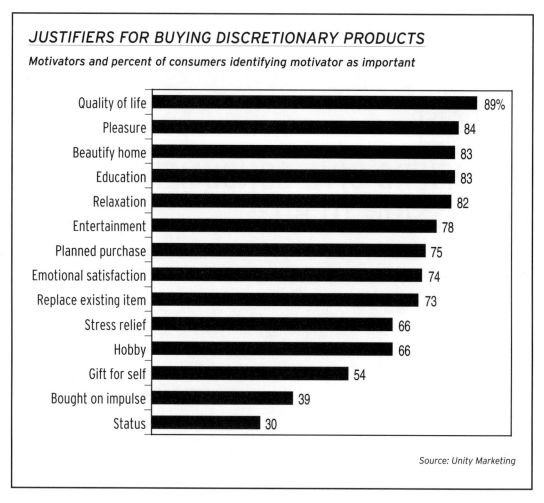

JUSTIFIERS FOR BUYING DISCRETIONARY PRODUCTS
Motivators and percent of consumers identifying motivator as important

Motivator	Percent
Quality of life	89%
Pleasure	84
Beautify home	83
Education	83
Relaxation	82
Entertainment	78
Planned purchase	75
Emotional satisfaction	74
Replace existing item	73
Stress relief	66
Hobby	66
Gift for self	54
Bought on impulse	39
Status	30

Source: Unity Marketing

really understand how their products play into the hearts and emotions of their customers, the judicious use of justifiers in marketing communications stacks the deck in the marketers' favor and gives consumers permission to buy.

UNDERLYING MOTIVATORS

In research conducted among consumers, Unity Marketing identified an array of 14 different justifiers that consumers perceive as the underlying motivators driving their purchase of products they don't need. Pleasure, education, emotional satisfaction, entertainment, relaxation, beautify home or self, replace an existing item, planned purchase, stress relief, hobby, gift for self, and status are among the reasons consumers use to justify discretionary purchases. However, you can sum up the most important justifier for all discretionary purchases in a single overriding concept: to enhance the quality of life. One respondent described her motivation in buying discretionary items as, "products that help me be more myself." As this definition implies, people buy these products to improve and enhance the quality of their lives in all realms and aspects of their being.

For marketers of products consumers don't need, the marketing and branding challenge is to figure out how their brands and the products they are trying to sell make people's lives more meaningful, satisfying, and better. With that insight, marketers can present and reinforce the quality-of-life-enhancing message surrounding the product or brand. Quality-of-life-enhancing messages are powerful. They provide the kinetic energy that overcomes consumer objections and drives consumers to buy. When marketers do the hard work of providing the justifiers for their customers, it is amazing how this bolsters product sales. Justifiers overcome objections and compel the consumer to buy.

JUSTIFIER #1 Quality of Life

Unity Marketing conducted a quantitative telephone survey of a statistically representative sample of 1,000 U.S. households to better understand the role of justifiers in the consumer's purchase decision. Consumers were asked about their purchase behavior in 30 different categories of discretionary and luxury products—those products people buy that they don't need. We will look at the results of the survey of product purchases in the next chapter. Here we focus on the critical role that justifiers play in motivating consumers to buy.

In the survey, we asked about the importance of 14 different justifiers for purchasing things that they don't need. Based upon their responses, the most important motivator driving the purchase of discretionary products was "To Improve the Quality of Life." Nearly 90 percent of those surveyed identified this as a "very important" or "somewhat important" motivator for their purchases in the 30 discretionary product categories. All other motivators, such as pleasure, beauty, entertainment, education, and stress relief, are implicit within the top motivator: Improving the Quality of Life.

Improving the quality of life works on different planes within the consumers' psyche. It is a deep concept that marketers need to explore for their particular products and brands. In that exploration, marketers gain tremendous insight into how shoppers perceive the products that they buy as "need fulfilling." Insights into how products enhance the quality of life result in positioning strategies that play back to customers' basic beliefs and values.

Our research uncovered five different dimensions on which consumer products improve and enhance the quality of consumers' lives.

INTELLECTUAL—At the intellectual level, education and knowledge are widely recognized as a principal means for individuals to improve the quality of their life. Education may make it possible for a person to find a better job with greater opportunity for advancement. Education is a tool that enables people to deal more effectively and productively with their world. In our survey, 60 percent of respondents ranked "Education" as a "Very Important" motivator in the purchase of discretionary products. Most notably, it is a prime motivator for home computer and book purchases.

PHYSICAL—Health and freedom from pain and disease are keys to enhanced quality of life. "If you have health, you have everything," is a common expression. A desire for good health drives consumption of vitamin and herbal supplements, nutritionally enhanced foods and drinks, exercise equipment, and health care. The physical component of quality of life also includes stamina and energy, comfort and safety, and freedom from physical danger. Purchases driven by this motivator include water and air filters, bottled water, home security systems, appliances, and new mattresses with special features. Following the terrorist attacks of 9/11, this motivator suddenly gained new importance as the threat of death through violence or biological and chemical attacks became a real possibility.

SPIRITUAL—People's relationship with God, or whatever name they give to a higher being, is a major source of comfort and security. Through the relationship, they have a means to deal effectively with the unknown, the loss of loved ones, and their own impending deaths. The spiritual component enables consumers to become part of the flow of history and to believe that they are not alone in dealing with the travails of life. Purchases that express spirituality include religious goods, books, and memorabilia. Some consumers may reflect their spirituality in the themes they collect such as Christmas and Easter holidays. The U.S. war on terrorism heightens the role spirituality plays in driving consumer behavior. Our enemies proclaim this as a "jihad," a holy war of their god against ours. While we do not play into the enemy's hand by buying this spin, the simple fact is that countries, societies, and people at war and in crisis call upon God to strengthen them and give them victory. As the saying goes, "There are no atheists in fox holes," and with our world at war, we will see more and more emphasis on spirituality as a source of strength through the difficult times ahead. "God Bless America" is the motto of this first 21st century war.

EMOTIONAL—While we know *things* cannot provide happiness, the act of buying gives many consumers deep emotional satisfaction. There is the buildup of anticipation in planning a discretionary purchase. One of our respondents described it this way: "You get satisfaction, and you're thrilled about where you've just been, and you plan the next one. Greater satisfaction builds more anticipation for the next time."

The emotional component includes the pleasures of love and happiness in the home, freedom from stress, and a home environment that relaxes and provides emotional security. The consumer good itself may not provide emotional satisfaction. However, it enhances and encourages such satisfaction in its acquisition and use. Examples are bath salts, candles, and beautiful home decorations.

Another respondent told us: "There is anticipation in the search for something wonderful, then stress, then ultimate satisfaction when the right purchase is made. Then you want to do it all over again." Products perceived as indulgences respond to the emotional level. In the post 9/11 world, consumers in crisis seek emotional succor and stress relief by purchasing products that promise to provide them.

SOCIAL—Our social connections and network of family, friends, and associates enhance quality of life. Our network confirms that we are not alone, that we belong. Success in the social milieu yields an enhanced quality of life and is one reason why status, that external representation of having achieved social success, is an important motivator for nearly one-third of respondents in our survey. Gift giving is another important aspect of the social component. Our society sanctions numerous gift-giving occasions, from the annual Christmas-shopping spree to birthdays and formal occasions such as weddings and anniversaries. Gifting confirms our sense of belonging and yields enhanced quality of life to both the giver and the recipient. As we learn to live with the threat of terrorist attacks, the need for belonging will grow. Home party plans and other forms of direct selling, friend to friend, are perfectly suited to trends at work in our culture today. Home entertaining will also benefit from the new environment.

Demographic Distinctions

All consumers are highly driven to make discretionary purchases as a means to improve the quality of their lives, but certain consumer segments are even more responsive to this desire. This justifier motivates both genders equally. However, consumers aged 25 to 34—those who are most likely to be in the midst of career and family building are the age segment that rates "Improving the Quality of Life" as the highest driver for purchases. Black Americans rate improving the quality of life more highly than whites and Hispanics. Households with two or more individuals are more concerned than people living alone about improving the quality of their lives through consumption. Moderate-income households place a greater emphasis on quality-of-life enhancement than do lower or higher-income households.

Finally, consumers who have completed their education, whether at the high-school or college level, place a greater importance on improving the quality of life. On the other hand, those with incomplete educational attainment, either high school or college, place less importance on quality of life. Presumably, those individuals who make the effort to complete their education at whatever level they decide is appropriate are more motivated by quality-of-life improvement.

JUSTIFIER #2 Pleasure

Some consumers derive pleasure in anticipating, acquiring, and owning a discretionary purchase. The entire buying cycle contributes to the joy. Advertisements stimulate desire that arouses fantasies in the mind about how the product will satisfy the desire. One of our survey respondents said, "When I see commercials for beauty products, I get caught up in the fantasy. Sometimes I buy the products in those fantasy commercials, then I feel good for a while. I am satisfied for a while, then it becomes ordinary again, and I want to go out and shop for something special again."

A central part of the consumer fantasy is the buildup of anticipation leading to the purchase. The anticipation makes the ultimate satisfaction that much greater. It also enhances the shopping experience.

Let us face facts. We derive pleasure in shopping at one store as opposed to another, even if we do not buy anything. Shopping at Wal-Mart is considered basic, ordinary, mundane, but shopping at stores like Bloomingdale's, Saks, or Neiman Marcus is a pleasure experience in and of itself. In the exclusive shopping venue, the illusion is that the well-dressed store clerks are there simply to satisfy the shoppers' whims. They ooh and aah when you try on something. They are honest if something does not look just right. They encourage you in the joy of shopping. In fact, the very best salespeople are so enthusiastic that they actually shop with you, rather than try to sell you something. Moreover, it is so much more fun shopping together than alone. A respondent explains, "When I am down in the dumps, shopping makes me feel better."

Pleasure as a driving force in consumer shopping is as much about the doing and experiencing (e.g., verb), as it is in the item or product bought (e.g., noun). No wonder that so many companies selling things that consumers don't need take control of the complete sales cycle, opening company-owned, dedicated stores to present and sell the brand. These companies recognize that consumers often derive as much pleasure from the brand in the act of acquiring a product as they do from owning it. Marketers that sell through independent retailers need to be vigilant that their brands are sold in a pleasure-focused way. Sales training and point-of-purchase marketing materials are a start, but it is clearly a challenge for a company whose products bring pleasure when the shopping experience does not.

Demographic Distinctions

Pleasure is equally important for men and women as a motivator for discretionary purchases. Younger-to-middle-aged consumers, aged 18 to 54, derive the most pleasure from their discretionary purchases. Consumers in this age range are far more likely than those aged 55 or older to rate pleasure as "very important" in their consumer choices. Moderate-to-high-income households feel entitled to gain pleasure from their purchases and, therefore, are highly motivated by this factor as well. Consumers who are married or live in two-person households are more highly motivated by pleasure than singles living alone.

Getting It Right

INTIMATE BRANDS
Devoted to sybaritic pleasure

With its three core brands, Victoria's Secret, personal-care retailer Bath & Body Works, and White Barn Candle Company, Intimate Brands is a $5.1 billion company that markets a magic formula of sophisticated adult pleasure to its customers. It's a formula that has worked beautifully, with the company nearly doubling in sales from 1995. CEO Leslie Wexner credits Intimate Brands success to its brands, "What has been working and winning and will continue to work and win as far into the future as I can see are brands. Powerful, compelling, multi-channel brands." The key to its brand magic is the company's intimate understanding of its customers and its dedication to consistently delivering on the brands' promises. Victoria's Secret targets

JUSTIFIER #3 | Beautify the Home

Making a beautiful home is a priority for the majority of consumers because it is central to a person's identity. As one survey respondent explained, "I am house proud. The house is the single biggest investment you will make in your lifetime and you want it to reflect the care and love you put into it." Another says, "You want the look of your home to reflect you."

The importance of the home is magnified for women who do not work outside the home. "As a stay-at-home mom, you don't have a job that you get reassurance from, that you are worth something—that boost you get from your work. You get that feeling from your house and how it looks. You end up doing the same job over and over again. It gets tedious, but if your house doesn't look good, you aren't doing your job as a woman and mother." Another woman explains, "The house and how it looks is your responsibility. It all gets down to a reflection on yourself." For about 80 percent of those surveyed, beautifying the home is an important motivator for buying things they don't need. For these consumers, the home—how it looks and how it is decorated—is a reflection of the individual's identity, values, and self.

women of all ages, body sizes, and shapes, with the promise that they can attract the passion and hold the interest of their man. While sex always sells, for women sex must come wrapped in romance. Victoria's Secret's 900 stores and its mail-order catalog are female friendly, promising sex appeal and romance in a decidely adult, but non-pornographic way. The catalog's voluptuous and beautiful models are non-threatening to the female consumer because, with a touch of genius on the part of the company, the catalog uses a regular crew of models with whom the reader becomes familiar. The company's Bath & Body Works brand works along the same lines as Victoria's Secret. Through the company's exclusive "lotions and potions," a woman can entice her man with soft, caressible skin and draw him with exotic and sensual fragrances. The brands are all about pampering and indulgence, sex and romance, beauty and the power to attract. These are potent, evocative brand messages. Wexner says, "What are the characteristics of the best brands? They are always clearly defined, with a strong emotional content. It's simple. People want the brand. They buy the aspiration, the look, the attitude. All of it."

Cleanliness in the home is another aspect of beautifying the home. A clean home is a beautiful home. As one respondent explained, "Bathrooms are made for the SOUL. That is where I go to relax. A clean bathroom is also critical. It has to be clean and stay clean." Utilitarian products often offer cleanliness as an essential benefit. Since "Cleanliness is next to Godliness," the consumer connection to cleanliness is very deep, almost spiritual.

Demographic Distinctions

While men value a beautiful home, women are more highly motivated to purchase products for home beautification. The more youthful consumers, those aged 25 to 44, are the most intensely interested in home beautification. Households making $35,000 or more annually consider beautifying the home a higher priority in purchasing decisions than do those living in lower-income households where it is viewed as of little or no importance in their purchase decisions. Single-person households are less motivated by beautifying their home than are consumers living in two-or-more-person households and those with children.

JUSTIFIER #4 Education

Being better educated, learning something new, gaining new insights, understanding, and skills is an important motivator in discretionary purchases for over 80 percent of those surveyed. It is worth noting that the more education Americans get, the more education they crave. Today's American consumer is more educated than ever before. As recently as 1980, only 16.2 percent of the adult population aged 25 and older had completed four years or more of college. By 1999, that percentage had risen to 25.2 percent. Achieving more education will continue to be a primary driver for important discretionary product segments, especially books, magazines, newsletters, computers and related hardware, software, art, and even entertainment products.

Researching a new purchase, getting educated about the product category, the available brands, and price points, comprises a part of the anticipation cycle that gives so much pleasure to consumers. One of our respondents explained the time-consuming process that her family went through to select the right model and to get all the right features on a new SUV. "We just bought a new Ford Expedition. We used the internet to learn about the different models, then went around to all the dealers, looking at the different models, to see which was right for us. Then, when we settled on the Expedition, we needed to do more research about the model and what features we wanted. For me, the search adds to the anticipation."

Demographic Distinctions

Women respond more strongly to education as a motivator for discretionary purchases than do men. Younger-to-middle-aged consumers, aged 25 to 54, rate education as more important than both those older than age 55, and the extremely young, aged 18 to 24. Consumers older than age 55, in particular, rate education as of little or no importance in their buying decisions. Unity Marketing predicts that the baby boomers who are just now entering their mid-50s will behave differently than the current generation of mature Americans (born prior to 1946) in terms of their desire for education. Boomers, the most educated generation in history, should continue to be ravenous consumers of products that incorporate an educational aspect. We also predict they will return to the classroom upon retirement or as their single-minded focus on career shifts. Black consumers give higher importance to education, suggesting that this market segment views education as a key to improved quality of life. In purchasing discretionary products, families with children place the highest emphasis on education.

JUSTIFIER #5 Relaxation

Achieving a state of relaxation is a key justifier for consumers in our hectic, over-scheduled world. Just as with the other justifiers that stimulate purchases, relaxation is not just inherent in the product bought, but in the whole shopping experience. Stores that are sensitive to the need for relaxation invite consumers to spend more time in them. Moreover, as Paco Underhill, in his book *Why We Buy: The Science of Shopping*, says, the longer shoppers spend in the store, the more they spend. Marketing relaxation products in a relaxing setting is the ticket for success.

Products that offer relaxation span a wide range including candles, home fragrance and aromatherapy products, nature and outdoor gardening, art, music, and bath lotions and potions. They tend to appeal to multiple senses just as candles illuminate, scent the room, and provide warmth. Shopping experiences that encourage relaxation also tend to be multi-sensory, offering an environment where scents, sounds, and lighting wrap the consumer in luxurious surroundings.

Demographic Distinctions

Relaxation is a closely related justifier to stress relief, which I will discuss later in this chapter. Relaxation is more multi-dimensional than stress relief and implies a broader, more life transforming, value than the stress relief justifier, which focuses on results. More than 80 percent of consumers rate relaxation an important motivator for discretionary purchases, whereas stress relief is important to only about two-thirds. While both genders are equally motivated by relaxation, women are more highly motivated by stress relief, suggesting that women need more of both relaxation and stress relief in their lives. Relaxation is more highly motivating to the middle-aged and older consumers; the prime age range for relaxation buying is 35-to-64. Blacks tend to view relaxation as a very important motivator, while whites are more likely to consider relaxation only somewhat impor-

Getting It Right

LONGABERGER BASKET
Education builds loyalty

As shoppers become more highly involved with a brand, a product, or a company, they seek out more information. Involved, passionate consumers want to learn and be educated, which results in better, more loyal consumers. The Longaberger Company, known for its handmade baskets sold exclusively through home parties hosted by the company's sales consultants, sponsors the Longaberger Homestead, near its headquarters in Newark, Ohio, dedi- cated to enhancing the consumers' experience of the brand.

Company founder Dave Longaberger envisioned the company facilities, which include a forest, golf course, and acres and acres of farm- land, becoming an educational and entertainment destination for visitors from around the world. The Longaberger Homestead combines down-home, country-style shopping, entertainment, and dining opportuni-

tant. Two-or-more-person households place a premium on relaxation in their discretionary purchases.

JUSTIFIER #6 *Entertainment*

Entertainment, as a powerful motivator for consumers, reduces boredom, generates excitement, provides new concepts and new ideas, and brings people together. American consumers spent $256.2 billion for recreation and entertainment in 2000, according to the U.S. Bureau of Economic Analysis. Americans have an unquenchable thirst to be entertained, with consumer spending on entertainment up nearly 50 percent from 1995.

As with so many other justifiers, entertainment is both what you buy and what you experience when you buy. "Shopping as entertainment" is a buzz phrase often heard in retailing circles. It has become so popular it has even spawned a new word; *retail-tainment*. The current trend in mall design includes combining traditional shops

ties with a tour of the manufacturing plant where people can experience, first-hand, the handcrafted traditions on which the company is founded. Visitors can even take a class where they make a basket themselves. Guests are also invited to tour the company's unique seven-story office building designed to look like one of its baskets, handles and all.

Thus, Longaberger becomes far more than a company that sells baskets.

- It involves and educates potential consumers.

- It invites the customer to become part of the

Longaberger experience for a few hours or a day.

- It presents the consumer with information about why their baskets are the absolute best.

- It builds loyalty, passion, and excitement for the brand.

Longaberger has made the quantum leap from a company trying to sell products to one that becomes part of the consumer's life. Educating the consumer with its Longaberger Homestead factory tours, sales consultant's presentations, and home parties is the foundation of the company's entire marketing and brand-building program. And it has worked spectacularly.

and anchor department stores with movie theaters, theme restaurants, museums, and other non-retail businesses. The Mall of America comes complete with an indoor amusement park featuring a full-sized Ferris wheel and roller coaster. The concept is sound. Consumers want to experience shopping in new, more dynamic ways.

Today's consumers ask more of their shopping entertainment. Not satisfied to passively receive entertainment, consumers seek a shopping experience that combines learning with doing to involve the complete individual. Speaking at the 2001 Urban Entertainment Development Conference sponsored by the Urban Land Institute, Mark Rivers, executive vice president of The Mills Corporation, explained that customers are drawn to shopping venues where they can participate in the excitement of entertainment. So The Mills Corporation, one of the nation's largest mall owners, worked with Vans Shoes to create skateboard parks and with Gibson Guitars to create places for people to play as well as purchase guitars. Rivers said, "The buzzword is experience. People do not want to just be enter-

Getting It Right

ABC CARPET & HOME
An oasis of luxury in the hustle-and-bustle of New York City

With the tagline, "Come to your senses at ABC," the ABC Carpet & Home store in the historic Flatiron District of New York, offers shoppers a truly one-of-a-kind shopping experience. Upon entering the doors of ABC's main building, the shopper is transported to an exotic world filled with wonderful things. The atmosphere is totally relaxing, luxurious, fascinating, and never-ever boring. ABC Carpet specializes in things for the home—rugs and carpets, furniture, antiques, home textiles, bedding, pillows, art, and collectibles. The experience is cocooning taken to extreme, spiced with objects from foreign locales and exotic places.

ABC describes its philosophy as NOT about decorating, but about collecting, "thus the process of creating one's home becomes less a makeover, and more a continual and passionate search to surround oneself with cherished belongings." The company carries out its mission in its merchandising philosophy. Its advertis-

tained. They want to participate. Creating these experiences is a good way to connect with consumers."

What people buy and how they buy it has become part of a total experience. Neither part of the consuming equation can be divorced from the other. That is one reason why The Limited's Structure stores ,which target the young male shopper, feature videos throughout the store playing music and fashion clips. Williams Sonoma offers cooking classes, while Home Depot will teach you how to install a sink, paint a room, or stain, clean, and even build a wood deck. The Disney Store plays Disney movies and cartoons around the clock. Big-box sporting-goods stores like Galyan's Trading Company, let the customer try out the goods before purchasing, even providing a three-story rock wall for the adventurous shopper to climb.

What's next in the one-upmanship world of retail-tainment? The sky is the limit. Be assured that consumers will be drawn to the next big thing in retailing that provides an entertaining respite from the drudgery of shopping.

ing describes it this way: " the ambiance of a flea market, a country antiques fair, a bustling Middle-Eastern bazaar and a bargain-filled warehouse sale, yet with the personalized attention one finds in a boutique."

Each of the store's ten floors is thematically arranged which offers the shopper a new shopping experience on each level. While the store is stacked and packed to the rafters with all kinds of merchandise, its atmosphere is anything but hectic. If you're feeling fatigued from wandering around such a phantasmagoria of home, you can rest and refresh in the food hall, featuring light fare, coffees and teas, pastries and other goodies. It even offers a full-course dining experience in its cafe featuring "Nuevo Latino" food. With cash registers respectfully dis-

creet, but sales help readily available, the store lives and breathes its philosophy.

In this eclectic mix of home items from all over the world, the store encourages its customers to "trust your impulses; create your own heirlooms; value will never go out of fashion." What could be more relaxing? ABC Carpet & Home has taken away all the worry of decorating, sorry...collecting, for your home. It gives permission to mix an embroidered coverlet with a Ming chair. "Introduce the second piece to the first, and eventually you will have an extended family of furnishings. This is collecting, not decorating." And the shopping experience underscores the message to "relax, enjoy, explore, collect."

Demographic Distinctions

Entertainment as a justifier for purchase is rated equally by men and women. All age groups are motivated by entertainment in their discretionary purchases, but the younger group, aged 18 to 34, rank it even higher than the older consumers, aged 35 to 64, as very important in their purchase decisions. Blacks are more likely to consider entertainment a very important motivator. Consumers living in households of two-or-more individuals and those with children place a premium on entertainment value in their purchases. Moderate-to-high-income households are more highly motivated by entertainment, as are consumers with at least some college.

JUSTIFIER #7 | *Planned Purchase*

Three-fourths of consumers say making a planned purchase is an important motivator for discretionary purchases. As we have seen, consumers build the anticipation of making a purchase through the

Getting It Right

ETHAN ALLEN
Make it affordable through easy monthly payments

Home-furnishings giant Ethan Allen knows that few customers wander into its company-owned stores without a plan. Furniture represents a major expenditure for most households, and consequently, it is frequently financed over time. As a vertically integrated home-furnishings company, Ethan Allen offers its exclusive brand of furniture in more than 300 company-owned stores supported by the company's own finance plan. The finance plan, introduced in 2001, was a cornerstone of the company's growth that year. The company's marketing strategy, bolstered by its finance program, encourages customers to purchase entire rooms of furniture and accessories, rather than one item at a time. It offers attractive interest rates over extended periods to make even the most expensive suite of furniture affordable to most families.

With the company's tactical marketing strategies in place, it launched a $70-million national advertising campaign to get the word out about the new affordable Ethan Allen furniture. The ad campaign, called "For Life," invites the consumer to participate in a fantasy of owning, using, and having great furniture. The ad highlights three specific products, each introduced with how important that piece of furniture is for your life. The Horizon's bed, priced at $949, is described, "You work on it...You think on it...You play on it...Spend all day on it." The Tribeca sofa, for $1,349, is to "Pass the time...Contemplate things...You

planning and research phases. Once this anticipatory phase is complete, the consumer has made the decision, stacked all the justifiers in favor of the purchase, and is now ready to make the purchase. Throughout what can be an extended planning period, excitement builds to the ultimate satisfaction of the purchase. "Anticipation is stress, healthy stress," a respondent explains. "You are excited, which is healthy, positive stress." Another explains, "the fun is in the looking." The opposite of planning a purchase is buying on impulse. Planning and anticipating a purchase tends to predominate in the consuming public, since only 40 percent of consumers claim that impulse is an important motivator for buying discretionary items. Shoppers

snooze...Watch TV...You rest on it..." The spot ends with "Ethan Allen. Furniture built for life...at a price you can actually live with."

This ad sends a powerful message that is perfect for our time. Your home, your furniture, your life means so much more to you now. It is the central focus of your life. Why should your furniture be an afterthought, bought quickly or cheaply? Enhance your life, add more meaning, more fulfillment, more comfort by buying the furniture you always dreamed of owning—Ethan Allen of course, now priced so even you can afford it. This ad breaks the mold in home furnishings because it is not about style, design, quality, or workmanship. It takes all those things for granted. What it does beautifully and convincingly is communicate at the emotional level. It almost turns plain furniture into a member of your family. It states, "You spend your life on it. Shouldn't it be the furniture you've always wanted?" What a powerful message.

This ad hit September 7, 2001, and its timing might well be fortuitous. During that awful time that followed the September 11 tragedy, we all craved comfort, support, nurture. This Ethan Allen ad was there to offer it through furniture. My guess: No other ad program launched during the troubled third and fourth quarter of 2001 has had such spectacular sales results.

who build anticipation toward a planned purchase perceive impulse shoppers as missing out on a lot of the fun in the consuming experience. As one shopper explained, "If you are an impulse shopper, you don't have any of [the fun]. There is no search, no anticipation. Sometimes the search can make you crazy, but I love it and love to buy."

Planning is a more important motivator for purchases that "cost" something, that is when the consumer has to give up something to make the purchase. Consumer durable purchases, those that are financed or usually paid for by credit card, take more planning to complete. The respondent we met earlier who was buying the Ford

Expedition described the decision to buy, "like deciding to have a new baby." It represented a major commitment of family resources over the five-year loan period, as well as increased operating expenses. Marketers of large-ticket items, which, for many families, require planning and budgeting, can often plan on an extended sales cycle that may be even further delayed due to minor shifts in the economic and political winds. In this post-9/11 time, consumers can put off major purchases for a few months or even a year until their personal prospects look more encouraging. On the other hand, some consumers may be overtaken with a "you can't live forever, so get it while you can" attitude that could spark extravagant purchases that would not otherwise be made.

Demographic Distinctions

Women tend to report making a planned purchase as a more important motivator than men. By comparison, men are more highly motivated by impulse purchases. Middle-aged consumers, aged 35 to 54, rate a planned purchase as more important to them than consumers under the age of 24 and consumers aged 55 and older. Two-or-more-person households and those with children are most likely to make a planned discretionary purchase. Single-person households place less importance on planning in their purchase decisions. College-educated consumers tend to rate planned purchases as more important, compared with less-educated consumers. An important aspect of the planning process in anticipation of a discretionary and luxury purchase is conducting research, something that the more educated consumers are better equipped to do.

JUSTIFIER #8 *Emotional Satisfaction*

Consumers buy things they don't need to achieve emotional comfort. It is the feeling of satisfaction, the gratification of having bought something desired, the happiness of purchasing something that perfectly expresses one's identity. It is the enjoyment of a beautiful home that provides safety and comfort to one's family and the challenge of being exposed to new ideas or learning new things. It is the fun of seeing the latest movie, playing the hit parade's top-selling song, or having the latest and greatest computer gadgets. It is exercising one's consuming will to buy and possess.

The art of branding is all about building an emotional connection with the consumer. While some categories are perceived as not demanding an emotional response from the consumer, no matter how mundane or low-involvement the product category, consumers usually are emotionally invested and connected with their favorite brands.

Remember the introduction of "New Coke?" It was so logical from a left-brain marketer's perspective, so carefully researched to find just the right combination of sweetness and tartness for today's taste. Yet cries of outrage from loyal consumers greeted New Coke. "How could you take away MY Coke?" The brand belongs to the consumers, not the company, and they own it in a visceral, emotional way.

This level of emotional involvement is the envy of all consumer brand marketers. Any brand manager who invests in understanding the emotional links between his brand and the consumers—their needs, drives, desires, consuming fantasies, and passion.—can achieve this level of emotional involvement for the brand. Few brands can span the breadth of a mass-market brand like Coke, but they can go equally as deep into their more narrow market segments by connecting with their customers on an emotional level and never letting them down.

Demographic Distinctions

Emotional satisfaction drives both men and women equally in discretionary spending. Consumers aged 25 to 54 are most influenced by emotional satisfaction in shopping. Consumers aged 65 and older are more likely than any other age group to claim that emotional satisfaction is of little or no importance when they shop. Blacks are more concerned with achieving emotional satisfaction through shopping, as compared with whites or Hispanics. Consumers living in large households of three or more individuals place a higher priority on emotional satisfaction as a reason to buy.

JUSTIFIER #9 | *Replacing An Existing Item*

The desire to replace an existing item in the home is often the justifier for the purchase of a discretionary item. In fact, this often becomes the catalyst for an extended spending spree. A worn-out chair, rug, or broken television is frequently the spur that moves buy-

Getting It Right

LENOX

Connecting emotionally at the most important times in people's lives

Hidden deep in the annual report of Brown-Forman, the wine and spirits company best known for its Jack Daniel's, Southern Comfort, and Korbel Champagne brands, is a tremendous marketing success story called Lenox. As the flagship brand of Brown-Forman's consumer durables segment, Lenox, along with other segment brands, including Gorham, Dansk, and Kirk Steiff in tabletop, Lenox Collections direct marketing, and Hartmann Luggage, posted a 16 percent increase in operating income in 2000 resulting from a 5 percent boost in net revenues to $592 million.

What accounts for the outstanding performance of the Lenox giftware brand? For starters, Lenox enjoys nearly a 40 percent share of the fine dinnerware market, thus assuring its position as the leader in the fine china business in the U.S. Further, Lenox's brand reputation has made it the dinnerware choice of the U.S. Presidents. Stan Krangel, president of Lenox Inc. boasts, "Lenox has delivered no fewer than five official sets of White House china for five Presidential administrations. The world's leaders dine on Lenox." Even more impressive, each and every citizen of this country participates in Lenox as one Lenox crystal bowl is given to each President as the official inaugural gift from the people of the United States.

The Lenox brand, however, extends far beyond market share dominance

ers from their homes and into the stores. Over and over in focus groups, respondents explained how the purchase of one item led to a cascade of additional spending to buy new things to complement and match the original item that started the spending spree. "We had an old chair. It cleaned up well but still looked dingy, so I went out and bought a new chair. Then when I got it home, it made the sofa and love seat look dingy, so we just replaced that. Next, I need to get new drapes, since the new furniture makes them look really bad." Another participant explains about her latest home spending spree, "We just bought four reclining chairs, including a couch with a recliner. We like to be comfortable, very comfortable. Now we need to get new things to go with [the couch]. One thing leads to another so you can justify new purchases. I've got to get a new rug. I wanted

and official gifts of state. Krangel explains, "Lenox is a brand consumers think of to commemorate the important celebrations in life—weddings, anniversaries, family holidays, new baby, showers, parties and entertaining, as well as more personal celebrations. Lenox serves the consumer at all these emotionally laden times of life. Lenox is a brand that people trust as a gift. For the gift giver, Lenox instills confidence in one of our most practiced rituals. For the recipient, Lenox represents appreciation of how much he or she is valued by the gift giver. Giving Lenox and owning Lenox represents American quality at its best."

With the core brand value of Lenox being "Lenox Gifts That Celebrate Life," the company targets distinctive areas in consumers' lives for their products. "Lenox's core equities are divided into four primary categories: Gifts, Entertaining and Mealtime, Home Decor, and Collecting. Each of these areas is driven by one form or another of celebration—the key emotional ingredient in Lenox's brand identity," Krangel says. "In essence, each of our core equities are forms of gift giving. Entertaining is one of the greatest gifts we share with our friends and families. Home decor and collecting are expressions and practices of self-giving. Lenox is the brand of choice for consumers' most special occasions."

The emotional connection fostered between Lenox and the consumer becomes the springboard to consumer loyalty. Lenox dinnerware patterns are designed to offer continuity at the table, as well as other giftware and decorative options. Lenox communicates with its customers through in-store support and displays, a Gold Club loyalty program, the company's internet websites, and consumer catalogs. The key message Lenox sends to the consumer, according to Krangel, is: "Lenox is here to help you celebrate again and again." What could be a better marketing strategy than to link up with consumers during all of their memorable life occasions?

new furniture for ten years, so now it is time to do it." A new backyard patio gives another respondent a justification to continue to spend: "We just finished the patio and sidewalk, so we needed plants to complement that. Then we needed patio furniture to complement that. It's a sense of accomplishment to show off what we've done."

Part of the motivation that drives the spending spree after replacing an existing item is to extend the thrill and excitement of having something new. Another respondent explained: "I always find myself buying bigger and better kitchen appliances. The kitchen is so important to me. I bought a new coffeepot with a water filter. The first time I used it I thought it was the best cup of coffee I ever made. I thought WOW! But now I just take it for granted. I just don't notice it anymore. Something new is a WOW. Improvements are amazing."

Demographic Distinctions

Women say replacing an existing item is a more important motivator for them to shop than do men. Older consumers, aged 45 to 64, consider this more important when they shop, compared with younger consumers aged 18 to 44. Moderate-income households rate replacing an existing item more important in their buying decisions than do households that are more affluent. Two-person and larger households are also more likely to consider replacing an existing item as an essential motivator to purchase.

JUSTIFIER #10 | Stress Relief

Finding a way to relieve stress motivates three-fourths of survey respondents in their discretionary purchases. Stress relief results from the act of shopping—from the relief and satisfaction felt upon culminating an anticipated purchase and from the product itself. Stress relief is an important benefit in the marketing of aromatherapy, candles, bath products, whirlpools, hot tubs, and small personal-care appliances.

In the post 9/11 terrorist-threatened world, consumers face an emotional crisis. Threats to personal security, when combined with economic uncertainty and rising global tension, create a feeling of stress for many Americans. When people are under stress, they fall back upon past behaviors that have proven successful in the past for relieving stress. In the aftermath of 9/11, some consumers turned to comfort foods. Others turned to the gym and strenuous activity for stress release or returned to old vices such as cigarettes and alcohol. Still others turned their feelings of stress into a justifier for more shopping.

When the crisis is long lasting or intensifies, stress relief will play a bigger role in shopping behavior. At the same time, consumers can cause themselves more stress by making expenditures they perceive as extravagant. Extravagance is in the eye of the beholder, but we can describe it as a purchase that a buyer cannot rationally justify. The higher the price, the harder consumers must work to find justifiers to give permission to make the purchase.

In the post 9/11 crisis, the sale of indulgence products, life's little luxuries that can be bought without guilt, will be vibrant for some time. Marketers and retailers need to be aware of new frugality taking hold in the American consumer characterized by a desire to get more perceived value for the money. Now is not the time to raise prices, but to look at ways to engineer products or find new suppliers in order to offer more indulgence value for a lower price. Promotions that focus on delivering more to the consumers, such as "two for the price of one" or "buy two get one free," are on target for today.

Consumers crave the comfort of traditions to relieve stress, so there is new demand for products that enhance and support family traditions. These include such things as Christmas and Hanukkah decorations, dinnerware for family get-togethers, kitchenware and kitchen decor, candles and fireplace or hearth products that "keep the home fires burning," and games and entertainment products that encourage high-quality family time. Back-to-basic toys give parents a chance to get down on the floor and play with their kids. Our holiday celebrations will hearken back to the past, as we try to recreate a Norman Rockwell Thanksgiving and a Victorian Christmas.

Suddenly "Made in America" becomes a much more potent positioning statement, as buying American is now a patriotic duty. While Americans accept products manufactured in foreign countries, they will look for foreign-made goods that are produced for an American company. They also may look at labels to find out where goods are made and reject products manufactured in perceived terrorist nations, including Indonesia. Be forewarned: if your company's products are manufactured in any of these countries, be prepared to change manufacturing sources fast.

Products that convey a symbolic or inspirational meaning will be in great demand, especially flags and patriotic-theme products. Do not expect consumers to lose interest in displaying, wearing, or flying the "red white and blue" soon. Inspirational themes, from "God Bless America" to angels, will attract more and more consumers as they seek peace in spiritual renewal. Bible sales, along with inspirational book titles, will see an upswing.

Nostalgia-theme products that recall a better, simpler time will bring comfort to consumers. Greeting cards, scrapbooks, diaries, and other products that enable personal communication will be in demand. Home will remain a focus of consumer spending, as consumers hunker down and try to make their homes a more secure and comforting environment. And keeping with the new economic equation, consumers will focus their home purchases on smaller accent and decorative items, as opposed to major appliances or furniture, which they will put off as long as possible.

Inevitably, consumers seeking stress relief are going to change their shopping patterns. They may retreat to the safety of their home. When they shop, they may want to spend less time at the store. They will do more of their weekly shopping in a single shopping trip. More shopping will be done from home, with consumers turning to the internet, mail-order catalogs, even party-based and other direct-selling businesses for their shopping needs.

Demographic Distinctions

Women are more strongly motivated than men by stress relief in their pursuit of discretionary products. Relaxation, a justifier closely aligned to stress relief, appeals more strongly than stress relief to both genders. Consumers aged 18 to 54 place a higher priority on stress relief. This justifier is not motivating to consumers aged 55 or older. Black consumers respond more strongly to stress relief in their discretionary purchases, while people living in households with two or more individuals consider it an important motivator for their purchases. Less-educated consumers feel more stress and seek relief more often in purchasing discretionary products.

JUSTIFIER #11 | Hobbies

Passion for a hobby is an important purchase justifier for two-thirds of consumers. Hobbies such as collecting, crafts, home workshops, photography, sports, and gardening drive many discretionary purchases. Collecting, for example, is a passion for over 40 percent of U.S. households, or in roughly 43 million homes. As "birds of a feather flock together," so do collectors, with an average of 1.7 collectors per collecting household. That makes about 73 million Americans passionately driven to collect.

The most popular collectibles include:

- *Coins, collected by an estimated 27 million Americans*
- *Figurines & sculpture, 20 million*
- *Trading cards, 18 million*
- *Memorabilia, 16 million*
- *Dolls, 16 million*
- *Christmas items, 15 million*

- *Plush/bean bag toys, 14 million*
- *Crystal figurines, 12 million*
- *Die-cast cars and models, 12 million*
- *Art prints and lithographs, 10 million*
- *Miniatures, 10 million*

The typical collecting household maintains more than three separate collections. Out of the 43 million collecting households, an estimated 70 percent purchased one or more items for their collection in the past year. With the typical collecting household spending $510 per year adding new items to their collection, that brings the total expenditure on collecting to about $16 billion in 2000, quite a sizeable amount of money spent on things people don't need.

The main reasons consumers collect include the joy of ownership and the thrill of the hunt. They also like the acquisition of a small luxury that brings pleasure without guilt, the achievement of special knowledge in an obscure subject area, and expression of identity, feelings, and values. As with all hobbies, the act of pursuing the hobby provides as much or more satisfaction and pleasure as that obtained in the completion of the hobby. For example, knitters and needlepointers enjoy the creation of their craft as much, if not more than, the actual object created. Exercisers and sports enthusiasts enjoy the playing, practicing, and working out as much or more than the toned, healthy body that results from their pastime. Collectors prize the search and hunt for the desired object as much or more as the new acquisition. One respondent explains his passion about collecting this way, "Don't you see? Collecting is all about the acquisition." He meant the act of acquiring (the verb), not the thing in and of itself (the noun). That is one reason why hobbyists like collectors are never finished. There is always some new challenge to pursue, some new desired object to find, something else to try.

Demographic Distinctions

Both genders are equally motivated by pursuit of a hobby in their discretionary purchases. Younger consumers, aged 18 to 44, are more likely to express importance of a hobby in their discretionary purchases. While collecting tends to be more actively pursued among middle-aged consumers, aged 35 to 64, younger consumers collect icons from their youth that they can find and trade on internet auction sites. By comparison, the oldest consumers, aged 65 and older,

Getting It Right

HALLMARK
The name is synonymous with gifts

As the nation's leading greeting-card company, Hallmark's brand image is intimately tied to gift giving. With sales of $4.3 billion in 2000 and holding 55 percent of the total U.S. greeting-card market, Hallmark defines its business as that of "personal expression." Hallmark continues to extend its brand into new areas that support its core mission including entertainment, the Binney & Smith Crayola brand, and even a corporate loyalty consulting business called Hallmark Loyalty Marketing Group. Since personal expression is a universal human need, the company maintains a global pres-ence with operations in more than 100 countries and product offerings in more than 30 different languages. It boasts domestic distribution through 47,000 retail outlets, including 39,500 mass merchandisers, discounters, and grocery stores, and 7,500 specialty stores, the pinnacle of which is its 4,800 Hallmark Gold Crown stores.

In essence, "why people buy" Hallmark is to express emotions. Don Hall Jr., the recently named president and CEO says, "These human needs to connect, communicate, and celebrate are enduring needs, which is why I have such confidence in the future of

are more likely than any other age group to say that a hobby is of no importance at all. Three-or-more-person households rate the interests of a hobby as an important motivator for their discretionary purchases.

JUSTIFIER #12 Gift For Self

How many of us go out shopping for a gift for someone else and come home with not one gift, but two—one for the person we went shopping for and one for ourselves? Usually the personal gift bought costs more than the gift for the other person. A consumer explained how personal gifting is pursued in the course of gift shopping for someone else, "One for you and two for me." The primary gift-giving occasions are Christmas and birthdays, followed in order by

our company." However, the way consumers express emotions is highly dependent upon the trends at work shifting and transforming the culture. Past Hallmark president Irv Hockaday explained it this way, "Hallmark doesn't look at itself so much as a greeting-card company as it does a company whose job it is to support and enhance relationships between people—parents, children, husbands, wives, friends, people in the workplace, and so on. Those needs I don't think are going to change. How our company responds to the needs is changing and will change."

To enable Hallmark to respond to the changing personal expression needs of consumers, Hallmark employs a trend expert, Marita Wesely-Clough, to head up the trend-tracking research team. Her job is to identify consumer trends as they emerge and help Hallmark prepare for the future. Wesely-Clough explains: "It's essential to stay close to consumers to know what is influencing the thoughts and feelings they want to express. We research emerging trends years ahead so that when people are comfortable reflecting new ideas and attitudes, Hallmark already has 'thought of that,' and exactly the right card is in the store."

While the company holds its "cards" close to the vest in terms of where its future lies, it does reveal it is actively investigating how it can take the "essence of the greeting card" into new arenas. John Breeder, vice president of greeting cards explains, "Hallmark also is expanding into areas that consumers give 'permission' for Hallmark to develop—where consumers trust Hallmark to provide solutions to help them communicate, connect, and celebrate."

Valentine's Day, weddings and anniversaries, Mother's Day, Father's Day, Easter, and other occasions, such as showers, etc. According to the Bureau of Labor Statistics, consumers made $121.9 billion in gift purchases for those living outside of the home in 1999. The average U.S. household spent $1,143 on gifts for those living outside the home, which amounted to about 3 percent of after-tax income. It is likely that significantly more is spent on gifts for those in the household. Gift spending corresponds to the relative closeness or distance in the relationship, except in the case of formal gift-giving occasions such as weddings. Thus, people spend more money on presents for children and spouses than on neighbors or work associates. In the case of formal gift-giving occasions such as weddings, consumers are far more likely to buy with an eye to status. Consequently, they will spend more on such gifts.

Getting It Right

OUTLET SHOPPING
Brand names at bargain prices

Serving the needs of impulse and value shoppers nationwide are the country's roughly 300 shopping centers that feature manufacturers' outlets. These bargain-oriented outlet malls attract consumers in search of brand-name products at a discount. Linda Humphers, editor-in-chief of *Value Retail News*, published by the International Council of Shopping Centers, explains, "From the customer's point of view, the ability to find a wide assortment of goods with well-known brand names, in a specialty store atmosphere with value pricing, is the major lure." The biggest draws in outlet shopping are the upper-tier brand names that are traditionally carried in department stores and specialty boutiques, like Ralph Lauren Polo, Liz Claiborne, and Brooks Brothers. These brand companies favor the control

Nevertheless, they spend the most on themselves. One consumer explains how she picks the best for herself, "That [speaking of a less fine item] is one I would give as a gift, but this is something I would keep for myself." The tendency to pick the best for yourself should not be attributed solely to selfishness. Most shoppers are far more attuned to what *they* like, as opposed to what *someone else* might like, so they are inclined to be more passionate about the gift intended for personal use.

Demographic Distinctions

Men and women are equally likely to indulge themselves in buying personal gifts. All age groups fall victim to this desire, except for the very oldest consumers, those older than age 65. Black consumers respond more highly to this tendency than other racial and ethnic groups. College graduates and those with post-graduate education are more likely than less-well-educated consumers to view giving a gift to oneself as an important motivator for discretionary purchases.

they get in inventory selection and brand image when they operate their own outlets. Humphers says, "Those in the outlet sector realize how much better it is to put overruns and past season's goods in an environment they control, rather than with a jobber or an off-price retailer that might jam designer goods onto broken hangers next to low-end merchandise."

Also a critical component in the outlet shopping experience is location. "Not to be underestimated is the location of many outlet centers in resorts, where time-deprived consumers can relax and take their leisure time to shop for bargains," Humphers adds.

Accounting for roughly $15 billion in annual sales, outlet shopping is still relatively small in the grand scheme of the nation's $3 trillion retail sector. Yet outlet malls exert a powerful pull on the shopper's psychology that goes beyond the right combination of price, selection, and quality. As Humphers states, "Since most of us rarely need anything we buy, outlet shoppers can justify their purchases as intelligent and sensible because they know the brands and they know what they're worth. Besides, we all like to think of ourselves as smart consumers, and smart consumers check out the outlets."

JUSTIFIER #13 *Impulse Purchase*

Buying on impulse is an important factor in discretionary purchases for about 40 percent of consumers. Based upon our survey, buying on impulse is about half as important as making a planned purchase. While the consumer who plans his or her purchase gains satisfaction from the emotional buildup and anticipation surrounding the upcoming purchase, the impulse shopper gains a sense of power and entitlement from making an impulse buy. One respondent explains: "I see something I like and I buy it. It's knowing that you are the one that got it. It gives me a feeling of power."

Sales are a powerful motivator for impulse purchases. Finding a good price or a bargain is the ultimate justifier for purchase, because it instantly takes away any guilt associated with making an unplanned, spontaneous purchase. "I like to save money," one consumer says. "If I can save money, I'll buy it, even if it is something I was just thinking of buying, but not necessarily at that time." Another consumer explains, "When I find something on sale, I feel like a winner." Feelings of guilt are a powerful de-motivator for buying something

Getting It Right

TIFFANY

Status in a robin's-egg-blue box

Today's ultimate gift comes wrapped in a robin's-egg-blue box with a white ribbon. What is inside? It doesn't really matter because the package says, "It's from Tiffany's," arguably the United States' most prestigious home-grown luxury brand, which has served the carriage trade since 1837. In fact, so much of the Tiffany brand's identity is tied up in its box that the company has registered trademarks for TIFFANY BLUE BOX and the color TIFFANY BLUE.

The company's stated mission is "about things that last," reflecting its timeless delivery of superior-quality products and service. With over three-fourths of the company's sales represented by jewelry, the company also offers a broad-based mix of luxury lifestyle products, notably timepieces, sterling silver, china, crystal, stationery, fragrances, and accessories. Its reputation as a premier luxury brand has been nurtured for over 165 years,

you don't need. A sale takes the guilt away, "I think if you buy something you don't need, you feel guilty, but if you find it on sale, then you feel less guilty," explains a consumer.

Demographic Distinctions

Men are more likely than women to buy discretionary products on impulse, thus destroying the illusion that men are the more rational shoppers. Younger consumers, especially those aged 18 to 24, are more likely to act on impulse in shopping than older consumers, especially those aged 55 or older. These more mature consumers are the most likely to rate impulse buying as of little or no importance in their purchase decisions. Consumers at lower income levels as well as those at the highest are most highly driven to make impulse purchases. Less-educated consumers also give impulse purchasing a higher priority.

when the company opened its first retail store in downtown Manhattan. Today, about 12 percent of the company's $1.6 billion in 2000 sales are credited to Tiffany's Fifth Avenue flagship store. Besides the company's flagship store, it operates 41 other U.S.-based retail establishments and has been undergoing worldwide expansion through over 75 international stores. Not satisfied to wait for the customer to come to them, Tiffany's also maintains an active direct-marketing program through the internet and catalogs. Its brand catalog was mailed to more than 1.2 million names in 2000. The Tiffany company views its brand expansively. The brand means more than simply products. It is about the experience of shopping in a wonderful environment "where exceptional products can be touched and where extraordinary service can be fully experienced," explains its 2000 annual report. While the company's hallmark is superior products and service, its strategies "have never been about fashion or luxury or excess," says the shareholders' letter from Chairman William Chaney and President/CEO Michael Kowalski. While brand identity is often thought of as a marketing concept, it also represents significant financial equity. *BusinessWeek* magazine values the Tiffany brand at $3.48 billion in 2001, placing it among the top 75 of the world's most valuable brands. That is a lot of money riding on a simple cardboard box of robin's-egg-blue.

JUSTIFIER #14 Status

Status, finally, is the least recognized justifier for discretionary purchases. In this "politically correct" era, less than one-third of consumers are willing to own up to status as important in making discretionary purchase decisions. Harvard University's Juliet Schor views America's preoccupation with shopping and buying as "competitive consumption." For her, buying things is all about status and class distinctions. I will not go that far, but our research clearly shows that the consumers surveyed understated status as a justifier in buying discretionary products. In focus groups, respondents describe status as feelings of envy that arise when someone else has something they desire. Consumers also express status through friends, family, neighbors, and associates whom they recognize as individuals who have "made it."

Status plays a more important role as a justifier in purchasing products that are visible to others, such as clothes, watches, cars, coats, and patio furniture. Status is of lesser importance for products that are less visible, such as mattresses, bedding, washing machines, and dryers. So the more visible the product is to the outside world, the more important, overall, the role of status in the purchase.

One consumer explained the role of status, "I collect Longaberger baskets. I must have a 100 or more. I just love them. For me, having Longaberger baskets are about making me feel good, not necessarily status. But when people come into my home and see how many baskets I have displayed, they say, 'Wow! Look at that.'" Another explains her passion for gardening as partly related to showing the garden off to her neighbors and friends: "I just spent $400 on plants, including six baskets for the front porch and more baskets for the fence. We have a huge yard and all the neighbors come to see the garden. From now until frost, there is always something new coming up. It is gorgeous. I love showing off my yard. It's not really status, but it is so cool to have people come around and see all the different plants. I like to spread my passion for gardening."

Demographic Distinctions

Status is a gender-neutral justifier, impacting men and women equally. Younger consumers, aged 18 to 34, are more likely than other age groups to say status is important in their discretionary purchasing. Black consumers view status as more important than do white or Hispanic consumers. Lower-to-moderate-income households are more involved with status as a motivator than higher-income households. Households with two or more individuals rate status as a more important motivator for their discretionary purchases.

ACTION PLAN | *Putting Justifiers to Work*

To move shoppers to action—that is to buy something they don't need—consumer marketers must provide sufficient justifiers to overcome barriers to purchase and give people a reason to buy. Because consumers buy products for many different reasons, marketers need to make sure all of those reasons are reflected back to the consumer at every point of contact, including advertising and point-of-purchase. Key for any marketer is to understand how a particular product improves the quality of the consumer's life. Marketers need to define the different dimensions on which the consumer derives satisfaction from their products. Then they must communicate the new quality-of-life value proposition clearly and effectively. The 14 justifiers examined in this chapter all play a part in driving the consumer to action. They may stimulate an impulse purchase with an attractive sales offer, capture more add-on sales as a consumer makes a major planned purchase, or offer stress relief and comfort through the products' use or the shopping experience. For discretionary and luxury purchases, consumer marketers and retailers need to stack the value equation in favor of the consumer, to break down barriers and encourage consumers to buy.

Here are some additional tips to encourage people to buy things they don't need:

> ### Justifiers work together to create a predisposition to buy.
> Consumers ultimately make the decision to buy in their hearts—at the emotional level—but they need justifiers to rationalize the purchase decision with their heads. All the rational justifiers in the world will not make customers buy things they really do not want. Marketers need to capture the attention of the customer, draw him or her emotionally into the product, help create personal fantasies about how life will be enhanced through ownership, and then provide rationally based justifiers that give permission to buy.

> ### As the consumer's purchase decision is multi-dimensional, so too must the justifiers be multi-dimensional.
> No single justifier works alone. Rather, they work together to encourage the consumer to buy. Marketers need to explore the comprehensive scope of how the product enhances the quality of the consumer's life. In my experience, company executives may think they know how their products enhance the quality of customers' lives, even when they have not done any research. However, rarely do they have a clue about the real emotional hot buttons that turn a desire into a need in the consumer's mind. You need to dig deeply into the consumer psyche to figure it out. It takes hard work and a commitment to consumer research. High-quality, highly intuitive consumer research is critical to uncover the full dimension of justifiers at work when consumers make a purchase decision. Focus groups, in-depth one-on-one interviews, and other qualitative

research methods are useful tools to find out the real reason why consumers are drawn to the product.

Discretionary product marketers compete against other companies and products within their class as well as across a wide range of product categories. Today's consumer can pick among many different products and services to achieve stress relief, relaxation, pleasure, and so forth. Marketers must work hard to make sure the consumer picks their product, not a competitor's. They need to view the competitive landscape horizontally, as well as vertically. With such stiff competition, no company that wants to grow and succeed can ignore the need to engage their consumers on an emotional level, to turn wants into needs, and win their hearts through effective marketing and communication.

Justifiers are even more important when marketing to women. Women as a rule are more frugal than men are. They are less willing to spend money on themselves, and when they do, they spend less money than men do. It takes more effort on the part of marketers to get women to open their pocketbooks and buy products they don't need. Therefore, in the marketing of products that appeal mainly to women, marketers need to work even harder in stacking the justifier equation in the consumer's favor. Women need more permission to buy, and justifiers are the secret.

Cascade effect offers opportunity for add-on purchases. One purchase often leads to another as the consumer uses the original purchase as a justifier for a cascade of additional purchases. Marketers and retailers can put this "cascade effect" to good use to spur additional sales. Opportunities abound to offer items in groupings, special-offer packages, and suites. Make these deals even more attractive by offering special-discount pricing to give the consumer one more reason to buy today. Look at ways to engineer products in order to offer more indulgence-value for a lower price. Promotions that focus on delivering more to the consumers, such as "two for the price of one" or "buy two get one free," are on target for today.

Chapter 5

WHAT THINGS PEOPLE BUY THAT THEY DON'T NEED

Now that we have explored why people buy things they don't need, let us look more closely at exactly what categories of discretionary products they are buying. For the past two years, Unity Marketing has conducted a nationwide survey of 1,000 U.S. households representing a statistical sample of the country's total population, thus providing statistically reliable and projectible information. This survey is also conducted the same week each year to provide reliable trend information. Further, we collected the data in the last week of August 2001 before the 9/11 tragedy and the resulting consumer turmoil. In all, 30 discretionary product categories were included in the annual survey, with a few product categories added in the last year. Only products, no services, were included in the survey, as our assumption is that most service purchases are by definition discretionary in nature. We intentionally excluded from the survey two product categories that represent important discretionary spending for many consumers—food and clothing. Because each of these categories includes some purchases that are considered essentials as well as those that are discretionary, it seems entirely too confusing for the survey respondents to differentiate for us.

CONSUMERS BOUGHT MORE DISCRETIONARY PRODUCTS IN 2001

Consumer purchase incidence of almost all categories of discretionary products jumped in 2001 over the previous year. Product categories that climbed the most include:

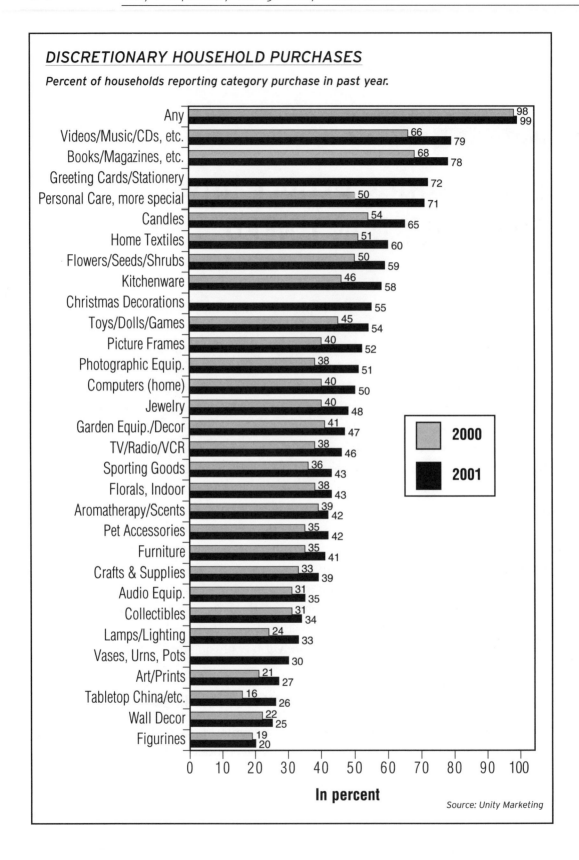

DISCRETIONARY HOUSEHOLD PURCHASES

Percent of households reporting category purchase in past year.

Category	2000	2001
Any	98	99
Videos/Music/CDs, etc.	66	79
Books/Magazines, etc.	68	78
Greeting Cards/Stationery		72
Personal Care, more special	50	71
Candles	54	65
Home Textiles	51	60
Flowers/Seeds/Shrubs	50	59
Kitchenware	46	58
Christmas Decorations		55
Toys/Dolls/Games	45	54
Picture Frames	40	52
Photographic Equip.	38	51
Computers (home)	40	50
Jewelry	40	48
Garden Equip./Decor	41	47
TV/Radio/VCR	38	46
Sporting Goods	36	43
Florals, Indoor	38	43
Aromatherapy/Scents	39	42
Pet Accessories	35	42
Furniture	35	41
Crafts & Supplies	33	39
Audio Equip.	31	35
Collectibles	31	34
Lamps/Lighting	24	33
Vases, Urns, Pots		30
Art/Prints	21	27
Tabletop China/etc.	16	26
Wall Decor	22	25
Figurines	19	20

In percent

Source: Unity Marketing

- Personal-care products, such as cosmetics, soaps, lotions, bath care, hair care, etc. that are more "special" or "exclusive" than the everyday brands, up from a 50 percent household purchase incidence in 2000 to 71 percent in 2001;

- Videotapes, music tapes, CDs, and, DVDs, up 13 percentage points from 66 percent household purchase incidence in 2000 to 79 percent in 2001;

- Photographic equipment and supplies, reaching 51 percent in 2001 from 38 percent in 2000;

- Kitchenware and accessories, rising 12 percentage points to 58 percent in 2001 from 46 percent in 2000;

- Picture frames (presumably to display all the new pictures being taken with the new photography equipment), up from 40 percent in 2000 to 52 percent in 2001; and

- Candles rising to 65 percent from 54 percent in 2000;

- Books, magazines, and newsletters, up from 68 percent in 2000 to 78 percent in 2001.

TOP-TEN DISCRETIONARY-PRODUCT CATEGORIES

Counting down the top-ten, discretionary-product categories by overall purchase incidence in 2001:

- Videotapes, music tapes and CDs, DVDs, etc,. bought by nearly 80 percent of U.S. households in the past year;

- Books, magazines, newsletters bought by 78 percent of households;

- Greeting cards and personal stationery, purchased by 72 percent of households.

- Personal-care products that are more "special" than the everyday brands were bought by 71 percent of households. This category moved up from 2000, jumping ahead of candles and home textiles;

- Candles, purchased by 65 percent of households;

- Home textiles, including rugs, throws, pillows, table linens, and curtains, bought by 60 percent of households surveyed;

- Flowers, seeds, shrubs, and trees for outdoor landscaping, with a purchase incidence of 59 percent;

- Kitchenware and accessories, purchased by 58 percent of households;

- Christmas and other seasonal decorations, with a purchase incidence of 55 percent; and

- Toys, dolls, and games, bought by 54 percent of households surveyed.

GENDER PREFERENCES IN DISCRETIONARY PRODUCT PURCHASES

Both men and women were surveyed about their households' purchase incidence of the 30 categories of discretionary products. The results indicate that some categories are more likely to be purchased by men, some by women, and some are unisex in appeal. The survey asked if "self or others in the household bought any product categories in the past year." We expect to find a higher purchase incidence reported by the gender that is primarily responsible for purchasing the item for the household. So for example, men are more involved with the purchase of computers (hardware and software), TVs, radio equipment, VCRs, etc.; sporting goods, exercise equipment and supplies; and audio equipment and stereo systems. Women reported a higher purchase incidence for books, magazines, and newsletters; greeting cards and personal stationery; personal-care products that are more "special" or "exclusive" than everyday brands; candles; picture frames; and crafts, craft supplies, sewing, knitting, and needlework. The rest of the categories have unisex appeal, as shown in the table.

GENERATION INFLUENCES DISCRETIONARY PURCHASE DECISIONS

Purchase incidence of most discretionary products drops with age, with the oldest consumers, the Swing and World-War-II generations (born before 1946), having the lowest overall purchase incidence. The younger generations, boomers (born 1946-1964) and Gen-Xers (born

PURCHASE INCIDENCE BY GENDER

Percent reporting purchase category in 2001.

Men	Men	Women
Computers, hardware and/or software for household use, not home office	54%	46%
TVs, radio equipment, VCRs	51	41
Sporting goods, exercise equipment and supplies	51	38
Audio equipment, stereo systems	41	29

Women		
Books, magazines, newsletters	75	81
Greeting cards or personal stationery	65	78
Personal-care products that are more "special" or "exclusive" than everyday brands	66	76
Candles	59	71
Picture frames	48	57
Crafts, craft supplies, sewing, knitting, and needlework	35	43

Unisex		
Videotapes, music tapes, and CDs, DVDs	80	78
Home textiles, including rugs, throws, pillows, table linens, curtains	59	60
Flowers, seeds, shrubs, and trees for outdoor landscaping	57	60
Kitchenware and accessories	59	58
Christmas decorations or other seasonal decorations	53	57
Toys, dolls, games	52	55
Jewelry	45	51
Garden equipment and decorative items for the garden or patio	48	45
Florals and greenery for indoor use	40	46
Aromatherapy or scented household products, such as potpourri, steamers	39	45
Pet accessories	42	42
Furniture	44	38
Collectibles	33	35
Lamps and accent lighting	33	33
Vases, urns, and pots	27	32
Art, prints, lithographs	27	26
Tabletop: china, crystal, silver, sterling flatware, and other dinnerware	24	27
Wall décor, such as sconces, mirrors, tapestries	26	24
Figurines and sculpture	18	21

after 1964), are the most active consumers of discretionary products, with the Gen-Xers being the most voracious consumers of most categories of products.

DISCRETIONARY HOUSEHOLD PURCHASES, BY GENERATION

Percent report category purchase in past year.

	Total	Gen-Xer	Boomer	WWII/Swing
Videos/music/CDs	79%	89%	86%	59%
Books, magazines, etc.	78	83	82	72
Greeting cards/stationery	72	71	74	71
Personal care, more special	71	79	71	73
Candles	65	88	71	52
Home textiles	60	64	64	48
Flowers/seeds/shrubs	59	51	64	61
Kitchenware	58	66	62	43
Christmas decorations	55	56	66	39
Toys/dolls/games	54	60	59	37
Picture frames	52	59	54	40
Photographic equipment	51	54	57	39
Computers (home)	50	58	56	31
Jewelry	48	56	52	35
Garden equipment/decor	47	45	53	38
TV/radio/VCR	46	56	48	30
Sporting goods	43	54	51	23
Florals, indoor	43	44	43	41
Aromatherapy/scents	42	53	45	25
Pet accessories	42	44	54	23
Furniture	41	52	43	24
Crafts and supplies	39	36	45	34
Audio equipment	35	46	38	17
Collectibles	34	39	38	26
Lamps/lighting	33	38	37	21
Vases, urns, pots	30	29	34	24
Art/prints	27	33	28	17
Tabletop/china/flatware	26	32	26	16
Wall décor	25	33	25	14
Figurines	20	22	23	13

Sources: Telephone survey, Unity Marketing

WILL BOOMERS ACT LIKE PREVIOUS GENERATIONS AS THEY APPROACH OLD AGE?

In the past, there has been a noted shift of consumer behavior after age 65, presumably due to a drop in personal income corresponding with retirement age. However, this pattern of reduced spending with age may not hold up as the baby-boom generation reaches age 65.

With the leading edge of the baby-boomer cohort turning 65 in 2011, that year may signal a drastic change in the fortunes of those consumer-product companies that sell things people don't need. On the other hand, every indication is that boomers have kept a youthful orientation that may well carry through the senior years without a drastic shift in their consumption behavior. Further, the age of 65 will not be the retirement benchmark it was for previous generations. Boomers' retirement age will extend to age 70, and those blessed with robust health and energy may work long after that.

Greeting cards and personal stationery, and florals and greenery for indoor use are the only two discretionary product categories that appeal equally strongly to all three generations. The personal-care category, including cosmetics, soaps, lotions, bath care, and hair care that are more "special" is also widely bought by all generations, but GenXers buy this category at a higher rate than other generations. Distinct generational patterns are observable in the purchase of all other discretionary product categories, as seen in the table above, with Gen-Xers and boomers buying at about the same rate in many categories.

In only a few discretionary categories do boomers lead in purchase incidence. The strongest boomer categories are flowers, seeds, shrubs and trees for outdoor landscaping; decorations for Christmas and other seasons; garden equipment and decorative items for gardens and patios; crafts and supplies; pet accessories; and vases, urns, and pots. The strongest categories for World-War-II and Swing-Generation households are books and magazines, stationery and greeting cards, and "special" personal-care items.

WHAT PEOPLE BUY:
Videotapes, music tapes and CDs, DVDs

In 2001, purchase incidence of videotapes, music tapes, CDs and DVDs rose to 79 percent of U.S. households, up from 66 percent in 2000. This makes videos, music, CDs, DVDs and tapes the most frequently purchased product people buy that they don't need.

Industry Snapshot

Total retail sales of pre-recorded videos and music reached $30.4 billion in 2000. Technological advances get credit for much of the recent growth in sales of this product category, especially the introduction of digital media for music and film recording. From 1997 to 2000, the installed base of DVD players in consumer households grew from 197,000 to 14 million homes. With more than 100 million households in the U.S., marketers of DVD players have only just begun to scratch the surface of their potential market. The Motion Picture Association of America (MPAA) reports that 182 million pre-recorded, DVD, software units were shipped in 2000, more than double 1999 shipments of 77.9 million. With an estimated average price of $25, the U.S. market for pre-recorded DVDs totaled $4.6 billion at retail in 2000.

As compared with the current installed base of DVD players, household penetration of VCRs is 86.1 percent of television-owning households, or 88.1 million households in 2000. Industry shipments of pre-recorded video cassettes for sale to consumers, as opposed to cassettes sold for the rental market, totaled 623.3 million in 2000, up from 620.1 million in 1999. With an estimated average retail price of $18, the total market for pre-recorded videocassettes was $11.2 billion in 2000, according to data from the MPAA.

Retail sales of recorded music on all media reached $14.3 billion in 2000, down 2 percent from 1999, according to the Recording Industry Association of America. Over 90 percent of the industry's sales are attributed to CDs. Rock-music sales have declined over the past decade, now accounting for only 25 percent of total industry sales, where rock commanded 35 percent of sales in 1991. Rap and Hip-Hop at 13 percent in 2000, and Pop music with 11 percent, have been

---

> ### PRE-RECORDED VIDEOS AND MUSIC
>
> *Sales in $ billions, 2000*
>
> DVDs $4.6
> Videos 11.2
> Music 14.6
> **Total** **30.4**
>
> *Sources: Motion Picture Association of America,*
> *Recording Industry Association of America, Unity Marketing*

gaining share, while country, now at 11 percent, and classical at 3 percent have slipped slightly from previous years.

Purchase Drivers

The added convenience of owning pre-recorded videos is an important driver for consumer purchases in this category. "I always forget to take our videos back to the rental store. I end up spending more on rental than I would if I just bought the tape," one focus group respondent confided. Besides convenience, many consumers want to keep up with technological advances, which bring better quality recordings and improved pleasure. Entertainment and pleasure are essential benefits this category provides. Music especially influences mood, so it offers emotion-moderating effects. Finally, children are major users of pre-recorded music and videos. For them, repeated watching and listening is a pleasure, whereas adults often get bored with frequent viewing.

Most families consider entertainment videos and recorded music an indulgence, but not too extravagant. The barriers against continued purchase of the category are falling as prices moderate, and the desire to save time and be more efficient makes buying, rather than renting a video or DVD, a more attractive option.

Demographic Variables

Purchase incidence of pre-recorded videos and music are on the rise, up from 66 percent of American households in 2000 to 79 percent in 2001. This is a gender-neutral category, with men and women reporting the same incidence of household purchase. While all ages buy pre-recorded videos and music, younger-to-middle-aged consumers (under age 54) are more active in this category. Households on the West Coast purchase pre-recorded videos and music more widely than in other regions. Middle-to-upper-income households are the prime targets for purchasing these products, as are households with children under age 18 in the home.

Households with higher levels of education are more likely to buy pre-recorded videos and music.

 KEY DEMOGRAPHICS FOR BUYERS OF PRE-RECORDED VIDEOS AND MUSIC

- *Gender neutral*
- *Young to middle-aged*
- *Middle-to-upper-income households*
- *Higher educational achievement*

WHAT PEOPLE BUY:
Books, Magazines, and Newsletters

With 78 percent of American households reporting the purchase of books, magazines and newsletters in 2001, this category is a very close second to pre-recorded videos and music as the most purchased product that people don't need. Purchase incidence was flat for this category compared with purchases in 2000.

Industry Snapshot

Retail sales of books and maps totaled $33.9 billion in 2000, up 10.4 percent over sales of $30.7 billion in 1999, according to the Bureau of Economic Analysis, Department of Commerce. Consumer sales of magazines, newspapers, and sheet music grew 11.8 percent to reach $36.8 billion in 2000, from $32.9 billion in 1999. As the population becomes more educated, expect demand for books, magazines, and newsletters to increase. At the same time, this category is facing competition from new technologies, most notably the internet, which more consumers are turning to for research, current events, and other personal information.

The way books and magazines are sold is also supporting sales growth in this category. Barnes & Noble and Borders have taken the concept of the small, private bookseller and completely overhauled it. They have introduced category-killer bookstores on a nationwide scale. They offer coffee, tea, and treats in a cafe setting, provide comfortable chairs so you can read as well as shop, and have expanded into music and videos in a more adult-friendly environment than the typical youth-oriented "record" store. The internet, too, is a powerful retailer of books, with amazon.com leading innovations in the category, and barnesandnoble.com and borders.com following behind, offering access to both in-print and out-of-print titles.

Purchase Drivers

Consumers are·motivated to buy books by many of the same things that favor the purchase of videos. They include convenience, saving time by not having to return books to the library, and personal and kids' entertainment. One consumer explains, "For me I always have

---

BOOKS, MAGAZINES, AND NEWSLETTERS
Sales in $ billions, 2000

	Sales
Books and maps	$33.9
Magazines, newspapers, sheet music	36.8
Total	70.7

Sources: U.S. Department of Commerce, Bureau of Economic Analysis

---

to have something to read. I read a lot and buy books everywhere. My friends ask me about using the library, but the library doesn't fit my schedule. I get a sense of desperation if I don't have a book to read."

However, at work in the motivation to purchase books is a unique emotional equation. Consumers are more personally and emotionally involved with their books than they are with videos and music. Part of a book's appeal may be that it is "low-tech"—one reason why so many industry pundits see little threat to the book publishing industry from e-books. Another factor may be simple nostalgia, since we all grew up reading books, holding books, striving to understand what was in books. For some consumers, this early exposure to reading never took off, but for others, books have become a very real and essential part of their lives. This emotional attachment to books is what makes them so collectible. In describing her library, a focus group respondent said "My husband and I love books and buy lots of books. Our house is full of bookshelves. I have a friend who thinks this is a luxury. She says, 'that is what libraries are for.' We go to the library, but I still buy books. They are MY books. It's about the pleasure of re-reading old 'friends.'" Another respondent wishes for a library to store all of her books, "I would love to have a library to keep all my books. Having a house with as many books as I have without a library is a challenge. I love books. I don't read every one, but I think in maybe a year or two I will get to them. I wish I had time to read all of them."

For most households, books and magazines are a personal indulgence, representing a small luxury that they can buy without guilt. For those with an inclination to buy books, the library is not a viable alternative. Consumers with a passion for books want to have a personal relationship with them and that requires ownership.

Demographic Variables

Seventy-eight percent of American households bought books, magazines, and newsletters in the past year. Demographically, women are slightly more likely to buy in this category, as are white/caucasian consumers. Younger-to-middle-aged consumers, aged 18 to 54, have the highest purchase incidence for books, magazines, and newsletters. Purchase incidence of these items also correlates with higher incomes. Households with incomes of $35,000 or more are the most active book buyers. Larger households of three or more individuals also buy books more actively. Like pre-recorded videos and music, purchase incidence correlates with educational levels. As educational attainment rises, so too does the household's purchase incidence for books.

 KEY DEMOGRAPHICS FOR BUYERS OF BOOKS, MAGAZINES, AND NEWSLETTERS

- *Female*
- *Primarily aged 18 to 54*
- *Middle-to-upper-income households*
- *Higher education achievement*

WHAT PEOPLE BUY:
Greeting cards and personal stationery

Just over 70 percent of American households purchased greeting cards and personal stationery in 2001. This makes greeting cards and stationery the third most frequently bought product that people don't need

Industry Snapshot

Total consumer retail sales of greeting cards and stationery, including school supplies, was $24.2 billion, up 7 percent over the previous year's consumer sales of $22.6 billion. This product segment has been both positively and negatively affected by the computer revolution. On the positive side, stationery suppliers have expanded their offerings to include cards and pre-printed stationery suited to use in computer printers. On the negative side, the ready availability of e-mail, as well as the continuing decline of long-distance telephone rates, predispose consumers to use more technologically advanced personal communication methods instead of old-fashioned "snail-mail" letters and greeting cards. Prospects for this market are mixed. The recent use of the mail system as a delivery method for biological terror puts traditional greeting cards and stationery at risk. On the other hand, the terrible loss of life experienced in our country from the tragedy of 9/11 encourages people to reach out to their loved ones and friends in ways they have not done in recent years. Therefore, the greeting-card industry stands to benefit from the need to express love and caring for others.

Purchase Drivers

Consumers use greeting cards both to accompany a gift and as a substitute for a gift. The industry has carefully honed its image with consumers through media advertisements. The industry positions a greeting card as a more thoughtful expression of feelings than a simple note. With illustrations and ready-made poetic sentiments, greeting cards help consumers convey emotions that they might otherwise find difficult to express. Recipients frequently keep greeting cards as reminders of the sender's sentiment. Given these advantages, the

---

GREETING CARDS AND STATIONERY

Sales in $ billions, 2000

	Sales
School supplies	$9.9
Greeting cards	7.5
Social stationery, invitations, etc.	6.8
Total	**$24.2**

Sources: U.S. Department of Commerce, Bureau of Economic Analysis; Greeting Card Association; Unity Marketing

---

industry positions its products as a far better way for consumers to connect emotionally with others. For the consumer, greeting cards and stationery offer real advantages, not the least of which are saving time and effort, since expressing deep emotions is difficult for many.

Demographic Variables

The greeting-card and stationery product category is a female-oriented category, with more women than men reporting a household-purchase incidence of greeting cards in the past year. Purchase incidence of cards and stationery cuts across all age ranges, but the highest overall purchase incidence is among consumers aged 45 to 54.

Purchase incidence of cards and stationery rises with income levels, with those at the highest income ranges, $50,000 or more per year, reporting the highest overall purchase rates. Neither children nor size of household has an apparent impact on the purchase incidence of greeting cards and stationery, but that purchase does correlate with educational attainment, with the more highly educated households purchasing in this category more frequently.

 KEY DEMOGRAPHICS FOR BUYERS OF GREETING CARDS AND STATIONERY

- *Female*
- *All ages, but 45 to 54 highest*
- *Middle-to-upper-income households*
- *Higher educational achievement*

WHAT PEOPLE BUY:
Personal-care products that are more "special" or "exclusive" than everyday brands

Purchase incidence of personal-care products that are more "special" or "exclusive" than everyday brands rose dramatically in 2001. Just over 70 percent of survey respondents reported that they, or someone else in their household, bought these "special" personal-care products, including cosmetics, soaps, lotions, and hair care. This category ranked as the fourth most frequently purchased discretionary product. Purchase incidence increased from 50 percent in 2000, suggesting that American consumers' involvement in the special personal-care category is growing rapidly.

Industry Snapshot

In 2000 the market for personal-care and cosmetic products grew 5.7 percent to reach $52.8 billion in retail sales, up from $49.9 billion the previous year. This jump follows 5.8 percent growth in this market from 1998 to 1999.

Purchase Drivers

Signs are positive for continued strong growth in this product category as people crave products like cosmetics and "lotions and potions" that pamper and indulge them. Even before the 9/11 crisis, consumers had a voracious appetite for the latest and most scientifically advanced personal-care and cosmetic products. The terrorist attacks accentuated trends favoring growth in special and exclusive personal-care products. Among the trends that have propelled growth in the personal-care and cosmetics industry is a search by aging baby boomers for cosmetics and beauty regimens that reverse the ravages of time. Changing fashion in makeup colors for the youthful consumer, the emergence of men as cosmetics users, and the demand for more product lines featuring natural, "healthy" ingredients are other trends that have had a positive impact.

Drawn like a moth to a flame, women cannot seem to get enough of this product category. One consumer explained her passion for perfumes this way, "I could wear a different perfume every day of the

SPECIAL PERSONAL-CARE PRODUCTS

Sales in $ billions, 2000

	Sales
Soaps	$5.4
Cosmetics/perfumes	19.2
Color cosmetics	10.3
Fragrances	8.8
Other toiletries	28.2
Hair care	7.9
Skin care	6.3
Bath and shower	4.1
Oral hygiene	4.0
Men's grooming	2.3
Deodorants	1.9
Sun care	1.0
Baby care	0.7
Total	**$52.8**

Sources: U.S. Bureau of the Census; Bureau of Economic Analysis; Unity Marketing estimates

year. I have so much perfume, but every time I smell a new fragrance I like, I have to buy it. I am addicted to scents." Another says, "I really go for bath gels and salts. It is a pleasure and a stress reducer. For me this isn't a reward. I am ENTITLED to have the nice 'stuff.' If we don't take care of ourselves, who is going to? Even with taking care of a large family, I have to have my hour in the bath."

Demographic Variables

The reported purchase incidence of special personal-care products is higher for women (76 percent) than for men (66 percent), but men are beginning to purchase more of these products for their own use. Younger consumers, under age 34, tend to have the highest purchase incidence for special personal-care products, but middle-aged folks, aged 35 to 64, also exhibit an elevated purchase incidence when compared with seniors aged 65 and older. This is a category where consumers living in metropolitan areas are more likely to buy than are their rural counterparts. People of all racial and ethnic groups purchase special personal-care products. Consumers living in households with average or above-average incomes are more likely to purchase special personal-care products than lower-income households are. Household size correlates with increased purchase incidence in the category, with larger households and those with children under age 18 purchasing more personal-care products.

 KEY DEMOGRAPHICS FOR BUYERS OF SPECIAL PERSONAL-CARE PRODUCTS

- *Under age 34, but remains high through age 64*
- *Middle-to-upper-income households*
- *Higher educational achievement*
- *All race and ethnic groups*
- *Urban more than rural*
- *Large households*
- *Households with children*
- *Female, but male share is growing*

WHAT PEOPLE BUY:
Candles

Sixty-five percent of U.S. households purchased candles in 2001, making candles the fifth most frequently purchased discretionary item. Purchase incidence rose from 2000 when about 54 percent of households bought candles. Even with this gain, candles dropped from the fourth most frequently purchased discretionary product in 2000 to the fifth most purchased in 2001, shifting rank with special personal-care products.

Industry Snapshot

Over the past five years, retail sales of candles have grown about 62 percent, rising from $1.5 billion in retail sales in 1996 to an estimated $2.4 billion in 2001. Early in 2001, slowing growth signaled that candle sales had reached their peak, but following the 9/11 tragedy, consumers re-energized the candle market as they surrounded themselves, at home, with the comforting, warm glow of candles. Continued broadening of retail distribution of candles is also supporting growth. Whereas five or so years ago the premium brands of candles were almost exclusively distributed in specialty-retail and gift boutiques, today 36 percent of total retail sales are generated among mass merchants, grocery, drug, and other mass-market outlets. Because of the entrance of mass merchants into candles, the specialty-retail channel has lost market share over the past two years.

Purchase Drivers

Candles represent an indulgence item that gives consumers an emotional lift and only costs pocket change to buy—the perfect antidote for fending off the blues. As a consumer product, candles are unique. Burning a candle has a magical, transforming effect. One focus group respondent said, "Every woman looks beautiful in candle light." Its flame mesmerizes, as this respondent describes, "I love to watch a candle burning. It's very relaxing to watch how they burn down." Its scent comforts and it sparks romance. Candles work on many different sensory levels to calm and refresh. A burning candle hearkens back to hearth and home. Candles are also a favorite gift item for hol-

---

CANDLES

Sales 1996-2000 and Projection 2001, in $ millions

	Total	**Change**
1996	$1,500	—
1997	1,800	20.0%
1998	2,100	16.6
1999	2,242	6.7
2000	2,314	3.2
2001	2,430	5.0

Source: Unity Marketing, The Candle Market, 2001

---

idays and throughout the year, as consumers seek gifts that will help them connect emotionally with loved ones and friends. One described the choice of candles as a perfect gift, "Everybody loves candles and you can get a really nice quality candle for $20 to $25, the price I like to spend on gifts."

Lighting a candle often signals a break from the ordinary and a time to relax. For some people, it is almost a ritual. A respondent explains that every time she sits down in her home office to work, she lights a candle. "I love candles and I always burn candles especially when I am working. When I light my candle on my desk, it means I am ready to work." Candles also support bathing and cleaning rituals, with a candlelit bath representing the ultimate in luxury. The fresh scent that candles impart in the home conveys cleanliness, "It reflects on your home, if it smells good. A burning candle gives a scent that tells how you keep your home and make it more enjoyable." For consumers, the role of scent in burning candles is very important, as three-fourths of all candles consumed are scented.

Demographic Variables

Women are more likely to report candle purchases for their home, with 71 percent saying they or someone in their household bought a candle in the past year. However, with 59 percent of men reporting the same, this is hardly a female-only category. Despite their lower overall reported purchase, men represent a market for candles as they both purchase and influence the purchase of candles, especially when romance is on the agenda.

Compared with those who live in the West and Midwest, consumers living in the Northeast and the South have a higher purchase incidence. Candles also appeal to all ethnic groups, with whites, blacks, and Hispanics buying candles at about the same pace.

As household income rises, so does candle purchase incidence. Consumers living in the most affluent homes, $50,000 or more, have the highest purchase incidence. Educational attainment also links to candle purchases. As education levels rise, so too does candle-purchase incidence. Larger households buy more candles, with two-or-more-person households and those with children buying more candles than people living alone.

 KEY DEMOGRAPHICS FOR BUYERS OF CANDLES

- *Female, but strong male participation*
- *No age discrimination*
- *Highest incomes, $50,000 or more*
- *All racial and ethnic groups*
- *Households with children*
- *Large households*
- *Higher educational attainment*
- *Northeastern and southern states*

WHAT PEOPLE BUY:
Home Textiles

The purchase incidence of home textiles, which includes rugs, throws, pillows, table linens, and curtains, rose from 51 percent in 2000 to 60 percent in 2001. Home textiles are an indispensable element of a well decorated home. Moreover, they pack the maximum decorating potential into an affordable bundle.

Industry Snapshot

In 2000, total household spending on home textiles and rugs was $48 billion, distributed as shown in the table. Changes in retail distribution of home textiles have contributed to growth in the category. The rise of national specialty retail chains focusing exclusively on home furnishings has attracted new consumer interest. Today, home furnishings stores generate nearly 30 percent of home textile sales. These stores include chains like Bed Bath & Beyond, a $2.4 billion group of over 300 stores headquartered in Union, New Jersey. Linens 'n Things trails the leader, with $1.6 billion in annual sales and 283 stores in 40 states, but it has led innovation in the category by offering a maximum selection of name-brand products at reduced prices. Other notable stores in this category include Kmart with its Martha Stewart Everyday line of home textiles; Target, with its reputation for being the most upscale of the discounters; and Tuesday Morning, an off-price retailer. These retailers are also attracting new consumers and siphoning away sales from traditional department stores.

Purchase Drivers

Rather than investing in major furniture pieces as they have in the past, consumers are buying more decorative accessories to change the décor of their homes. Home textiles, including rugs, throws, pillows, table linens, and curtains, offer an affordable, fun way to update the home. With the ready availability of name-brand textiles at discount prices, many consumers view new sheets, pillowcases, comforters, and duvets for their bedroom as indulgences, rather than major expenditures. "I have an addiction to decorating any room. I especially like TJ Maxx or Marshall's, where I can find a lot of really good

---

HOME TEXTILES

Sales in $ billions, 2000

	Sales
Towels, etc.	$3.9
Comforters, quilts	3.6
Sheets, pillowcases	3.3
Curtains and draperies	3.2
Blankets, pillows, mattress pads	2.5
Artificial flowers	2.3
Foam/plastic home furnishings	1.6
Bedspreads.	1.4
Bamboo, rattan	0.8
Table linens	0.6
Shower/bath curtains	0.5
Flags, banners	0.7
Shoe bags, laundry bags	0.1
Other furnishings	4.7
Total rug	19.2
Carpet, rugs, etc.	17.5
Pad liners	1.7
Total	**$48.0**

Source: Bureau of Economic Analysis, U.S. Department of Commerce
Note: Numbers may not add to total due to rounding

---

deals. I just bought a great rug on sale at TJ Maxx. I wasn't looking for it specifically, but I saw it and had to have it," one focus group respondent told us.

Demographic Variables

Men and women are about equal in their reporting of a home-textile purchase in the past year, suggesting that men and women are equally involved in the purchase decision for home textiles. All age groups through age 54 maintain a fairly strong purchase incidence, peaking among households aged 25 to 34, corresponding with the household-formation years, and those aged 45 to 54, associated with the empty-nesting period.

Middle-to-upper-income households with incomes of $35,000 or more are most active in this category. Household size and presence of children in the home correlates with increased purchase incidence, as larger households and those with children buy more frequently.

KEY DEMOGRAPHICS FOR BUYERS OF HOME TEXTILES

- *Men and women equally involved*
- *Peak ages 25 to 34 and 45 to 54*
- *Middle-to-upper income*
- *Large households*
- *Households with children*

WHAT PEOPLE BUY:
Flowers, seeds, shrubs, and trees for outdoor landscaping

Nearly 60 percent of American households reported buying flowers, seeds, shrubs, and trees for outdoor landscaping in the past year, up from 50 percent in 2000. Outdoor gardening is a passion for many. The Lifestyle Market Analyst 2000, from SRDS and The Polk Company, found that flower gardening ranks among the top-ten lifestyle activities in the U.S. Some 40 percent of U.S. households participate in this activity, trailing only a handful of other lifestyle activities.

Industry Snapshot

Consumer spending on flowers, seeds, and potted plants totaled $17.5 billion in 2000, according to the Bureau of Economic Analysis. However, that statistic tells only part of the story of America's passion for gardening. The National Gardening Association estimates that Americans spent $33.5 billion in total on all expenditures related to their lawn and garden. Two categories account for about half of total consumer garden spending: lawn care, totaling $9 billion or a 27 percent share, and landscaping, accounting for $8.6 billion or a 26 percent share.

Purchase Drivers

Gardening demands physical labor and therefore is a great way to relieve stress. As one focus group respondent explains, "Gardening is my husband's stress relief. Every year he puts in a garden, and it saves his sanity. He likes to work in the yard." Besides offering exercise, gardening appeals to people because it makes their yards look better, more attractive, and more inviting. Another respondent who is devoted to her yard says, "I love showing off my yard. I love to have friends over and to eat on the patio. I like them to admire my garden. I like to get praise and appreciation for my work and for them to recognize my accomplishment. Gardening is hard work." For some, maintaining their yard to the standards of the neighborhood is a factor, but most do it solely for personal enjoyment. Another respondent explains, "I just bought a lilac bush. I have always loved lilac—it's my favorite fragrance. Of course, it will make my yard look nicer, but I

U.S. LAWN AND GARDEN RETAIL SALES

Sales in $ billions, 2000

	1998	1999	Change
Lawn care	$8.5	$9.0	5.2%
Flower gardening	4.0	4.0	0.3
Indoor plants	1.2	1.3	9.6
Vegetable gardening	2.0	2.6	29.4
Shrub care	1.6	1.4	(15.8)
Insect control	1.7	1.2	(27.3)
Flower bulbs	0.6	0.6	13.5
Tree care	1.7	1.7	(0.1)
Landscaping	6.4	8.6	33.4
Fruit trees	0.3	0.3	(12.3)
Raising transplants	0.2	0.3	88.8
Container gardening	0.7	1.0	30.3
Growing berries	0.1	0.1	6.1
Ornamental gardening	0.3	0.5	39.3
Herb gardening	0.1	0.2	26.7
Water gardening	0.7	0.8	22.3
Total	**30.2**	**33.5**	**11.0**

Source: National Gardening Association, 1999-2000 National Gardening Survey

---

bought it for me." Another says, "I grew up on a farm, so I look at gardening as a necessity. It gives pleasure, relieves stress. After all, your house has to look as good as everyone else's in the neighborhood."

However, what can be stress relieving for one can be stress inducing for another. Some view the need to keep their yard up with their neighbors' yards as one more obligation: "I find it stressful. It is something I have to do, and it has to get done. It's not something I want to do."

Demographic Variables

With about 59 percent of households reporting they bought flowers, seeds, shrubs, and trees for outdoor landscaping in the past year, men and women participate in gardening purchases about equally. This is a category where the purchase incidence rises with age. Those aged 45 to 64 purchase more for their gardens than younger consumers, but purchases start to pick up at age 35 corresponding with increased home-ownership. Rising incomes, education levels, and household size all correlate with rising purchase incidence for the garden.

 KEY DEMOGRAPHICS FOR BUYERS OF GARDENING SUPPLIES

- *Men and women equally involved*
- *Peak ages 45 to 64, begins to rise at about age 35*
- *Upper income*
- *Homeownership*
- *Households with 2 or more people*
- *Higher educational levels*

WHAT PEOPLE BUY:
Kitchenware and accessories

Fifty-eight percent of U.S. households reported buying kitchenware and houseware accessories in 2001, up from 50 percent in the previous year. Spending on kitchenware and other housewares corresponds to consumers' emphasis on the home. The National Housewares Manufacturing Association estimates that the average American household spent $40 in this category in 1999, including plastic and foam kitchenware, kitchen utensils, cookware, cutlery, and non-electric cookware.

Industry Snapshot

Total spending on kitchenware and housewares was $27 billion in 2000, up from $25.1 billion in 1999. That represents a 7.6 percent increase in spending on kitchenware products not classified as consumer durables. The single largest segment in the housewares category is plastic and foam kitchen accessories and housewares, accounting for a remarkable 60 percent of total sales in the category, at $16.2 billion. This category includes buckets, baskets, storage, throwaway drink cups, plates, and containers of all other kinds. The second most widely sold item in housewares is metal cooking and baking utensils, totaling $5.8 billion in sales or 22 percent of the total market.

Purchase Drivers

Often viewed as a necessity rather than a discretionary purchase, a significant amount of spending on kitchenware is for storage containers to store all the other unnecessary "stuff" people buy, accumulate, and collect. Along with a clean house, people crave an organized house. As one focus group respondent explained, "With all the men [i.e., husband and three sons] in my house, everything is a mess. I would love to have it better organized. There would be less stress if it was better organized. Right now, it is all ripped apart."

In servicing the need to store the things we buy, Newell-Rubbermaid, a $6.9 billion company, which generates nearly 70 percent of total company sales in housewares products, is on to

---

KITCHEN AND HOUSEWARES

Total sales in $ billions, 2000

	Sales	Share of Market
Plastic and foam kitchen and housewares	$16.2	60.1%
Aluminum/stainless cooking and baking utensils	5.8	21.5
Wooden housewares	2.4	8.8
Vacuum, insulated, and canning	1.2	4.6
Cutlery	0.7	2.6
Other	0.7	2.5
Total	**27.0**	**100.0**

Sources: U.S. Census Bureau, Bureau of Economic Analysis

---

something. The company has been uniquely successful at taking generic everyday housewares and making them more special, more highly positioned, more in demand among consumers, through branding. Their housewares brand portfolio includes Rubbermaid, Levolor, Calaphon, Pyrex, and Kirsch. The company has moved upmarket in recent acquisitions, such as Paper Mate/Parker, Burnes of Boston, Graco, and Little Tikes. It has added more exclusive brands to its portfolio, signaling a strategic move and growing awareness that company growth will come from selling to satisfy consumers' emotional, rather than physical and practical, needs.

Demographic Variables

A gender-neutral category, equal shares of men and women report purchasing kitchenware and housewares accessories. Younger consumers under age 45 are the leading buyers in this category, while purchase incidence drops sharply after age 65. Purchase incidence rises along with household income, with the strongest market segments being those with household incomes of $35,000 or more. Household size and presence of children in the home correlate with purchase incidence, as the larger households and those with children under age 18 in the home express a greater need to buy kitchenware and other housewares.

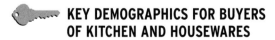 **KEY DEMOGRAPHICS FOR BUYERS OF KITCHEN AND HOUSEWARES**

- *Men and women equally involved*

- *Trend toward under age 45*
- *Incidence rises with income*
- *Larger households*
- *Presence of children*

WHAT PEOPLE BUY:
Christmas decorations and other seasonal decorations

Christmas is the pinnacle of all holiday decorating, though because of Martha Stewart's and other home-decorating mavens' tutoring, Americans have expanded the number of holidays for which they go "all out" and decorate their house. More than half of American households (55 percent) purchased Christmas decorations or other seasonal decorations in the past year, up from 50 percent in the previous year. While no statistics are available about the exact number of homes that decorate for each major holiday, the holidays that are key for home decorating are Valentine's Day, Easter, Fourth of July, Halloween, Thanksgiving, and, of course, Christmas.

Industry Overview

Christmas-holiday-decoration sales totaled $6.4 billion in 2000, including sales of ornaments, artificial and live/cut Christmas tees, Christmas lights, and other party or holiday goods. The U.S. Census Bureau estimates that China is the number-one source for ornaments, lights, and artificial Christmas trees sold in the United States. The Christmas tree is the center of holiday decorating in most American households. The National Christmas Tree Association estimated that 82.5 million households would decorate with a tree in the 2001 holiday season. Some 32.3 million families would purchase a live or cut tree as their holiday centerpiece. Only about 7.3 million households planned to purchase a new artificial tree in 2001.

The passion with which we decorate and celebrate the Christmas season is a uniquely American phenomenon. Department 56's Judith Price, director of collector relations, explains, "When you go to Europe, even to our Canadian neighbors to the north, you don't see the extravagant outdoor displays or the kind of over-the-top gift giving that we experience here in the States. The way we celebrate Christmas is a purely American holiday and reflects the blending of so many other cultures' traditions that have been brought over by wave after wave of immigrants." Department 56 is a $250 million company that has staked its fortunes on the uniquely American Christmas cele-

---

CHRISTMAS DECORATIONS, RETAIL SALES

Sales in $ millions, 2000

	Sales
Christmas tree ornaments total	.$2,724.6
Collectibles	623.6
Tree and trim	2,101.0
Artificial Christmas trees	1,491.9
Cut/live Christmas trees	1,098.0
Christmas lights (indoor and outdoor)	729.6
Party and holiday goods	375.6
Total	**6,419.7**

Sources: Bureau of Economic Analysis, Census of Import Trade,
National Christmas Tree Association, Unity Marketing

bration. Best known for its elaborate lighted villages, the company also sells a full range of Christmas ornaments and trim.

Purchase Drivers

Christmas decorating is a much-loved family tradition. While some families go in for the full outdoor display, others center their decorating on the hearth and tree. Bringing out the holiday decorations usually marks the "official" beginning of a family's holiday celebration. Many families maintain a collection of ornaments and decorations for years, annually adding new items to their collection to mark the passage of each year.

Nostalgia for Christmas past is a key driver for purchases of new items used to decorate. Consumers want to re-create those special celebrations remembered from childhood. Tapping into this trend for nostalgia, the Christopher Radko company is reintroducing the Shiny Brite line of ornaments, recreating vintage Christmas decorations produced in the 1940s and 1950s. Shiny Brite was first made by Corning before World War II. The latest versions will hail from China, based upon vintage designs. A string of authentic bubble-lights, rarely seen today but remembered from the childhood of many boomers, will cap the new collection.

Demographic Variables

Women tend to take the lead in holiday decorating traditions, so purchase incidence of Christmas and other seasonal decorations is higher among women than men. Purchase incidence of Christmas decorations peaks between the ages of 35 and 54, after beginning to rise from ages 25 to 34. Regionally, households living in the North Central states (e.g., Illinois, Indiana, Michigan, Ohio, Iowa, Kansas, Minnesota, Nebraska, North Dakota, and South Dakota) report the highest purchase incidence.

No racial diversity exists in the purchase of Christmas decorations. Higher-income households tend to purchase more decorations that are seasonal. Household size and the presence of children in the home correlates with purchasing decorations. Larger households and those with children have a much higher purchase incidence of Christmas decorations.

 KEY DEMOGRAPHICS FOR BUYERS OF HOLIDAY DECORATIONS
- *Peaks between ages 35 and 54, begins among 25-to-34-year-olds*
- *Larger households*
- *Presence of children*
- *Female-led category*

WHAT PEOPLE BUY:
Toys, dolls, and games

Fifty-four percent of U.S. households purchased toys, dolls, and games in 2001, up from 45 percent in 2000. While children represent the core-user market for toys, more adults are buying toys, not just for kids, but for their own playtime, too. Toys are popular adult collectibles, and more toy companies are recognizing that adults, just like their kids, want to play with toys.

Industry Snapshot

The toy industry is a nearly $29 billion industry at retail, up 8.5 percent over 1999 levels of $26.4 billion. Notoriously given to boom-and-bust cycles, the toy industry's fastest-growing categories in 2000 were ride-on toys, such as skateboards, scooters, and other riding toys, sales of which were up 66 percent, reaching $1.5 billion. Other growth categories were infant and preschool, reaching $2.4 billion in sales on 24 percent growth; and activity toys, including building sets, scientific sets, craft kits, crayons, markers, and model kits, rising 17 percent to $3.1 billion in sales.

TOY RETAIL SALES ESTIMATES, BY CATEGORY

Sales in $ billions

	1999 Sales	Market Share	2000 Sales	Market Share	Change 1999–2000
Video games	$6.5	24.7%	$6.8	23.8%	4.7%
Activity toys	2.6	10.0	3.1	10.8	17.4
Dolls	2.6	9.8	3.0	10.5	15.7
Infant/preschool	1.9	7.3	2.4	8.3	23.8
Vehicles	2.0	7.7	2.3	8.2	15.1
Games/puzzles	2.1	7.8	2.2	7.7	6.8
Plush	2.9	10.8	2.1	7.2	(27.6)
Ride-ons	0.9	3.5	1.5	5.3	65.5
Action figures	1.3	5.1	1.1	3.8	(18.4)
All others	3.5	13.4	4.1	14.4	17.2
Total	$26.4	100.0	28.6	100.0	8.5

Sources: Unity Marketing, Bureau of Economic Analysis, Toy Industry Association

HOUSEHOLD PROJECTIONS, 2000–2010

(in millions of households)

Age group	2000	2005	2010	Growth Trend 2000–2010
18–24	5.9	5.4	5.7	(3.4)
25–34	18.8	16.6	17.5	(6.9)
35–44	24.0	22.6	20.6	(14.2)
45–54	20.2	23.9	25.3	25.2
55–64	13.6	17.3	20.7	52.2
65+	21.6	23.1	25.1	16.2
Total	104.1	108.9	114.9	10.4

Source: U.S. Bureau of the Census

Purchase Drivers

American parents cannot do enough for their kids! That is the simple reason behind the steady growth in the toy market. The toy industry enjoyed many years of growth as the baby-boom generation progressed through its prime childbearing years. However, in 2001, with the leading edge of the baby-boom generation reaching age 55 and the trailing edge now at age 37, the toy industry faces hard times as the much smaller Generation-X enters its family formation and childbearing years. The total number of households under age 45 will decline from 2000 to 2010, down 3.4 percent in the group aged 18 to 24, 6.9 percent for the group aged 25 to 34, and 14 percent for the group aged 35 to 44.

Demographic Variables

The most significant demographic variable favoring toy purchases is the presence of children in the home. Three-quarters of households with kids bought toys in the past year. Men and women report about equal purchases in the category, suggesting that both genders are equally involved in the purchase of toys for their homes. Householders aged 35 to 44 are the largest consumers of toys, with 64 percent in that age range reporting the purchase of toys. Unfortunately for the toy industry, this is the very age group that will decline the most from 2000 to 2010. Purchase incidence is also elevated among households aged 18 to 34. Unlike many other categories, the purchase incidence of toys is not highly dependent upon household income, with 55 percent of households in the income range $25,000 to less than $35,000 purchasing items in the category.

 **KEY DEMOGRAPHICS FOR BUYERS
OF TOYS, DOLLS, AND GAMES**

- *Gender neutral*
- *Peaks in ages 35 to 44, but also high for 18 to 34*
- *Not dependent on income*
- *Presence of children*

WHAT PEOPLE BUY:
Picture frames

In 2001, the purchase incidence of picture frames among American households rose from 40 percent in 2000 to 52 percent. With more people interested in displaying family pictures in their homes and offices, the picture-frame industry has responded by offering new designs in frames that add visual interest and contribute to the over-all presentation. Appreciative consumers are spending more on picture frames.

Industry Snapshot

Gift picture frames, intended to frame snapshots and smaller pictures, and sold mainly in gift shops and gift departments of mass merchants, represented over a $1 billion market in 2000. Sales of gift picture frames grew from $988 million in 1998 to $1.3 billion in 2000, a 36 percent increase, according to Unity Marketing's *Gifts & Decorative Accessories Report*, 2001.

Purchase Drivers

Who doesn't have pictures of family and friends displayed on their mantel, end tables, or book shelves? Picture frames satisfy a universal need for people to create personal momentos and remembrances. Until fairly recently, the focus of picture-frame manufacturers was to simply "frame" a picture, with the picture being the center of atten-tion. However, a few years ago, picture-frame companies discovered that the frame itself could add interest to the display and started to offer more fashionable, stylized frames. Consumers gobbled them up as they found that distinctive frames added value to their prized and cherished pictures.

Demographic Variables

With purchase incidence of frames on the rise, the demographic pro-file of the picture-frame consumer skews toward young women. With a reported household purchase incidence of 57 percent, women are more likely than men to take the lead in purchasing frames for their homes. Only 48 percent of men report the purchase of frames for their household. Purchase incidence is highest among the most youthful households, aged 18 to 34. However, purchase incidence remains strong among 35-to-64-year-olds, and drops sharply after age 65.

Rising income correlates with rising picture-frame-purchasing incidence, with purchasing highest among households with incomes $35,000 and above. The presence of children in the home has only a small impact on the purchase incidence of picture frames, with 50 percent of households without children purchasing compared with 56 percent of those with children. However, multiple-person households are far more likely than single-person homes to purchase picture frames. Fifty-five percent of two-person households and 54 percent of three-or-more-person households purchase frames. In single-person homes, only 41 percent report buying picture frames.

 KEY DEMOGRAPHICS FOR BUYERS OF PICTURE FRAMES
- *More likely to be female*
- *Rises with rising income*
- *Multi-person households buy more*
- *Younger households, aged 18 to 34*
- *Not dependent on presence of children*

WHAT PEOPLE BUY:
Photographic equipment and supplies

Purchase incidence of photographic equipment and supplies is on the rise, climbing from 38 percent in 2000 to 51 percent in 2001. The significant increase in purchase incidence relates directly to new technology and the ready availability of affordable digital cameras. Digital cameras with their ability to store and arrange picture images on computer disks are an attractive and lasting alternative to record a family's heritage, rather than flimsy paper images stuffed in books, drawers, and scrapbooks.

Industry Snapshot

Sales of photographic equipment topped $4.5 billion in 2000, up 8.6 percent over industry sales of $4.2 billion in 1999. The market for photographic equipment is vibrant and benefiting from technological advancements, such as digital imaging and computer storage of digital images. No longer is the family or hobbyist photographer limited to storing images on film or paper. Today, photographs are being stored as digital images on computer files, thus opening a whole realm of new possibilities in photography storage and transmission.

Purchase Drivers

Driving the purchase of new photographic equipment is innovation in technology. With the price of digital cameras coming down and more households having access to a computer, consumers want to upgrade their old cameras with the latest digital models. As one young mother explains, "I really wanted a digital camera. I asked my husband for one for my birthday, but I knew he wouldn't get it. So I went out and bought it for myself. I want to record all the stages of growth of my baby. It's important, but my husband doesn't see it like I do."

Demographic Variables

A gender-neutral category, men and women report about the same level of household purchasing of photographic equipment and supplies. Households headed by persons under age 55 reported the highest purchase incidence of photographic equipment in 2001,

---

SALES OF PHOTOGRAPHIC EQUIPMENT

Sales, in $ billions

	Sales	**Change**
1998	$3.8	—
1999	42.0	9.0%
2000	4.5	8.7

Source: Bureau of Economic Analysis

---

suggesting that the younger consumers' greater familiarity with computers and all things technological favors purchases in this category.

Middle-to-upper-income households have a far higher purchase incidence of photographic equipment and supplies than lower-income households. Over 60 percent of households with incomes of $35,000 or more purchased in this category in the past year. Increased household size and the presence of children in the home also link to higher purchase levels. One-half of households with two people and 58 percent of those with three or more members reported purchasing, while 60 percent of households with children, compared with 45 percent without, bought photographic equipment in 2001. Higher educational levels also correspond to purchase incidence, as households with at least some college purchased at a much higher incidence than high school-educated households.

 KEY DEMOGRAPHICS FOR BUYERS OF PHOTOGRAPHIC EQUIPMENT

- *Gender neutral*
- *Rises with income and education*
- *Households under age 55*
- *Larger households and those with children*

WHAT PEOPLE BUY:
Computers, hardware, and software for home use (Not home office)

The purchase of computers, hardware, and software for household use, rather than for use in a home office, rose from 40 percent in 2000 to 50 percent in 2001. Consumers are buying their first computers or upgrading to the latest models as desktop computer prices reach levels of $1,000 or less. Householders also are adding new software and hardware accessories to handle photography files, music recordings, and household records. Seemingly, the appetite for the latest computer technology is unquenchable.

Industry Snapshot

The U.S. Bureau of Economic Analysis reports personal consumption of computers, peripherals, and software totaled $34.3 billion in 2000, up 9 percent over 1999 sales levels of $31.4 billion. As long as the computer industry continues to feed the consuming public's desire for the latest and greatest computer technology, sales should continue to rise. The percent of households with a computer reached 51 percent in 2000, up from 42 percent in 1999. Nearly 42 percent of households now have access to the internet, according to the Census Bureau. With 49 percent of households still without a computer, there is room for growth in the U.S. home-computer market. In addition, the need for computer hardware and software upgrades among the 51 percent of households that are already computer-equipped portends a strong market.

Purchase Drivers

The need to upgrade an existing home computer is a key driver for new-computer buying. As one recent computer purchaser explained, "We just bought a computer. We already had one, but it was about 300 years old in computer years. We needed a faster computer. Now with the new computer, if I wanted to work at home, I could." Another consumer purchased a second home computer with the plan that this machine will last for a few more years. "We just bought a computer. This was our second computer. I could have lived with the old com-

---

**COMPUTERS, PERIPHERALS AND SOFTWARE
FOR HOME (NOT HOME-OFFICE) USE**

Sales, in $ billions

	Sales	Change
1998	28.7	—
1999	31.4	9.4%
2000	34.3	9.2

Source: Bureau of Economic Analysis

---

puter, but I wanted a new one. I hope we don't have to upgrade it anytime soon, so we got all the bells and whistles. We even added surround-sound speakers."

In buying new computers, consumers are looking for expanded functionality—the ability to do something with the computer they never could do before, positioning computers squarely as a utilitarian discretionary purchase. As one respondent put it,"We just bought a new lap-top computer. We didn't strictly need it, since we have three others at home already. But we needed the laptop because of changes at my work. I have to drag things back and forth for work so the laptop is a real convenience."

Often, the educational needs of children justify computer purchases. In our research, one parent told us, "A basic computer is almost a necessity today, especially for the kids who have to do research on the internet and write papers. The educational component of the computer is very important. Your kids have to keep up."

Once the computer is in the home, consumers often want to upgrade their machines to add capabilities and functionality. Another respondent said, "We added a CD burner to our computer so we can pick and choose the songs we listen to. The reason I purchased the CD burner is because we recently suffered a number of deaths in my immediate family. It made us realize that life is too short. You should have fun. If something gives you pleasure, then you should enjoy it. We deserve it, and it makes you a better person and a more pleasant person to be around. Music is important to our family, and now we can do custom mixing, so we enjoy life more."

Demographic Variables

Men take the lead in household computer purchases, with 54 percent of men reporting the purchase of a computer, software, or hardware for home use, as opposed to 46 percent of women. Youthful house-holds, especially those aged 55 or younger, are more likely to have purchased a computer or related equipment in the past year. However, 46 percent of households headed by persons aged 55 to 64 bought a computer in the past year, suggesting that the perceived need for a computer is spreading in the mature market as well. White and Hispanic households are more likely to purchase computers than are black households.

Middle-to-upper-income households are far more likely to have bought a computer, with purchase incidence exceeding 60 percent for households with income greater than $35,000. Computer purchase is also strongly linked to the presence of children in the home; 63 percent of households with children, compared with only 41 percent of those without, reported buying a computer and related equipment in 2001. Households with "some college" and those with more educational attainment are much more likely to purchase computers.

 KEY DEMOGRAPHICS FOR BUYERS OF COMPUTERS, HARDWARE, AND SOFTWARE FOR HOME USE

- *More likely men*
- *White and Hispanic more likely than black*
- *Presence of children favors purchase*
- *More educated households*
- *Households under age 55, but strong even among households aged 55 to 64*
- *Income levels of $35,000 and above*

WHAT PEOPLE BUY:
Jewelry

More households bought jewelry in 2001 than in 2000. Purchase incidence of jewelry rose from 40 percent in 2000 to 48 percent in 2001. Contributing to the growth in the jewelry market is the expanding availability of jewelry at the retail level. In 2000 Wal-Mart was the nation's largest jewelry retailer, with over $2 billion in jewelry sales.

Industry Snapshot

Total sales of jewelry and watches were $51.4 billion in 2000, up 6 percent over the previous year's sales of $48.5 billion, according to statistics collected by the Bureau of Economic Analysis. Because of the economic slowdown throughout 2001 and the terrorist attacks in September of that year, we predict the sale of the luxury category of jewelry and watches will slow, as consumers struggle to justify purchases that are more extravagant. On the other hand, mass market jewelry, especially costume jewelry, was expected to remain vibrant through the 2001 sales year, as consumers buy less-precious jewelry for an emotional lift.

Purchase Drivers

Jewelry is a favorite indulgence item for women, especially as a fashion accessory. Jewelry, especially fine jewelry, is also a favored gift item for men to give women on ceremonial occasions such as weddings and anniversaries, as well as birthdays, Christmas, Valentine's and Mother's Day. Moreover, women are prone to give themselves a gift of jewelry when they need a boost, as one woman clarifies, "I bought a bracelet for myself on my birthday. I spent $5,000 at Neiman-Marcus buying a bracelet that I always wanted. For my birthday, my husband took me out to dinner at a restaurant not far from where I bought the bracelet. He thought [dinner out] was all I was getting. But I felt I deserved it now."

With rings given to celebrate marriage, jewelry carries a more symbolic meaning than many other discretionary items as one young respondent explains, "I like to shop for jewelry. There are so many things connected with jewelry, like Christmas and the birth of a child.

JEWELRY AND WATCHES

Sales, in $ billions

	Sales	**Change**
1998	$44.3	—
1999	48.5	9.6%
2000	5.4	6.0

Source: Bureau of Economic Analysis

It is symbolic and meaningful to someone. I have lots of nice jewelry that I will pass down to my daughters." Another respondent explained that, often, it is the symbolic meaning of a jewelry item that drives its purchase: "I was in Toronto and found an emerald ring in an antique shop. I had to buy it. It took me back. It was nostalgic, fulfilling a desire I have had for 20 years to own a ring like that. I will always associate that ring with Toronto. At the time, I was making memories, as well as enjoying them."

Demographic Variables

With a purchase incidence of 51 percent, women are just slightly more likely than men (45 percent) to have purchased jewelry in 2001. The core market for jewelry is more youthful, with households younger than age 55 reporting the highest purchase incidence. Householders aged 18 to 24 purchase the most, with an incidence of 66 percent.

While households at all income levels buy jewelry, those at the highest level, $50,000 and above, report the highest purchase incidence (59 percent). Household size and presence of children in the home is linked to jewelry purchase incidence, with larger households and those with children buying more jewelry.

 KEY DEMOGRAPHICS FOR BUYERS OF JEWELRY

- *Women buy slightly more than men*
- *High-income households, $50,000 plus*
- *Households under age 55*
- *Larger households and those with children*

WHAT PEOPLE BUY:
Garden equipment and decorative items for the garden and patio

With consumers, especially homeowners in the group aged 35 to 64, spending more money on landscaping and on their lawns, it is not surprising the purchase incidence of garden equipment, furniture, and decoratives is going up as well. Purchase incidence for equipment, furniture, and decorative items for the garden was 47 percent in 2001, up from 41 percent in 2000.

Industry Snapshot

In 2000, U.S. consumers spent $5 billion on garden equipment, furniture, and decoratives. Lawn and garden furniture spending totaled $2.3 billion, including $253 million on wooden furniture and $2 billion on metal outdoor furniture. Equipment classified as consumer durables (e.g., push and riding lawn mowers, snowblowers, and other major equipment, but not including hand tools) reached $1.8 billion in sales. Garden decoratives, including flags, sculptures, birdbaths, birdhouses, birdfeeders, and other outdoor decorations totaled $1 billion at retail.

Purchase Drivers

Spending on one category for the home frequently results in additional spending in other categories, justified by the original purchase. It is no different with consumers' spending on the garden. The upgrade of plants, landscaping, or the lawn often results in the purchase of garden equipment, furniture, and decorations to match the new, improved, outdoor look. As one consumer explained, "We just put in a finished patio and new sidewalk, so we needed plants to complement that. Then we needed patio furniture to complement that. It gives me a feeling of accomplishment."

Grills are a frequently named utilitarian purchase for the garden, with the grill giving the owner a new way to cook. One woman told us, "My husband is crazy about grills. We already have four grills. The gas grill is for me because I love the convenience and don't want to build a fire. My husband likes to cook regularly and use hickory. Now he wants to buy a smoker, not just one, but two, so one smoker can

---

SALES OF OUTDOOR LAWN EQUIPMENT, FURNITURE AND GARDEN DECORATIVES

Sales in $ billions, 2000

Porch, lawn, beach, and similar wood furniture $0.3
Metal porch, lawn, outdoor furniture 2.0
Garden decoratives 1.0
Garden and lawn equipment (mowers, snowblowers) 1.8
Total **5.1**

Sources: Bureau of Economic Analysis, Unity
Marketing Gifts & Decorative Accessories Report 2001

---

be at home and another one at the campground. I think we have enough already. I ask him how often he will use a smoker. Once a year is what I say, so why buy two?"

Demographic Variables

Men and women report about the same purchase incidence of garden equipment and accessories, suggesting that both men and women are equally involved with such purchases. Like the purchase of outdoor plants and landscaping, the purchase incidence is highest among more mature households, aged 35 to 64. Purchase incidence of garden equipment and accessories peaks among the 45-to-54-year-olds. While there are no meaningful regional differences in purchase incidence, white households are more likely to purchase than blacks.

Purchase incidence is concentrated among the middle-to-upper-income ranges. Homeownership seems to be an important link. Purchase incidence is highest among those with incomes of $50,000 or more. Larger households and those with children are more likely to buy garden equipment and accessories than single-person households and those without children.

 KEY DEMOGRAPHICS FOR BUYERS OF LAWN AND GARDEN EQUIPMENT

- *Gender neutral*
- *Households with incomes of $50,000 or more*
- *Highest among households aged 45 to 54*
- *Larger households and those with children*
- *White households more likely than black households*

WHAT PEOPLE BUY:
TVs, radio equipment, and VCRs

Most television purchases, even purchases of VCRs, are to replace or upgrade existing equipment. Nearly all (99 percent) of U.S. households own a color television, while 67 percent own two or more TVs. VCR ownership is almost as high, with 88 percent of households having a video recording machine. Today the digital DVD is being used more and more as a video recording medium, thus encouraging consumers to upgrade their older VCR player for the latest and greatest digital DVD player. In 2001, 46 percent of households reported making a purchase of a TV, radio, VCR, or other video equipment, compared with 38 percent in 2000.

Industry Snapshot

In 2000, personal consumption of VCRs, DVDs, and recording media such as videotapes, exceeded spending on TV sets that display video media. Spending on VCRs, DVDs, etc. totaled $28 billion, while spending on television sets was $20.3 billion.

Purchase Drivers

Like computers, technological innovation in the recording and display of video images is a major driver for growth. DVDs are rapidly replacing video cassettes as the recording medium of choice for video images, thus motivating U.S. households to upgrade their video playback equipment to be compatible with DVDs. Television too is changing with digital technology. The new flat-screen television display technology brings improved display of digitally stored images, as well as cable and satellite digital transmission. Consumers are also buying wide-screen television sets, enhanced with new sound technology that projects such a large image that they can recreate a movie theater experience in their own homes. As one focus group respondent explained, "My husband just bought a wide screen television set. It was actually a practical purchase since we have had two television sets stolen in the past. My husband bought the big wide-screen television because thieves wouldn't be able to get it out the door. We also have the only wide-screen television in the neighborhood, so it is a

---

SALES OF TVS, DVD PLAYERS, AND VIDEO EQUIPMENT

Sales in $ billions, 2000

Televisions	$20.3
Other video equipment (VCR, DVD, tapes, etc.)	28.0
Total	**$48.3**

Source: Bureau of Economic Analysis

WOW when people come over. My husband likes to watch sports." I suspect that television thieves have mastered the skill of stealing the much more expensive large wide-screen television sets, but this wife seemed convinced that her husband was making a practical decision when he bought the new set to enjoy the football games and show off to his friends.

Demographic Variables

Men are largely responsible for the purchase of televisions and video recording equipment for their households. More than half (51 percent) of men, compared with 41 percent of women, report purchasing this equipment for their homes in 2001. Younger consumer households, under age 45, have the highest purchase incidence of televisions, VCRs, etc. Perhaps the skew toward younger consumers is due to the widely recognized "fact" that those older than age 45 cannot program a VCR. While these more mature consumers have adapted quite well to the computer, the VCR machine remains off limits to the technically challenged. Surely, with a little attention to the end user, the video player manufacturers could expand their market quite effectively.

In buying televisions and other equipment, black households lead whites. Higher-income households, especially those with incomes of $50,000 or more, have the highest purchase incidence in the category. Purchase incidence links to household size and presence of children in the home, with two-or-more-person households buying more than one-person households, and those with children more likely to buy than those with no children.

 KEY DEMOGRAPHICS FOR BUYERS OF TVS, VCRS, AND DVDS

- *Male-led category*

- *Highest-income households buy most*
- *Households under age 45*
- *Larger households and those with children*
- *Black households buy more*

WHAT PEOPLE BUY:
Sporting goods, exercise equipment, and supplies

Reported purchase incidence of sporting goods, exercise equipment, and supplies rose to 44 percent in 2001, from 36 percent of households in 2000. Exercise walking was the sport in which the most people participated during 2000, according to the National Sporting Goods Association. More than 86.3 million Americans aged 7 or older walked for exercise at least once. Other popular sports were swimming, 60.7 million; camping vacation overnight, 49.9 million; fishing, 49.3 million; and exercise with equipment, 44.8 million. The fastest-growing sports, based upon participation, are snowboarding, up 31 percent, and skateboarding, up 30 percent in total participation.

Industry Snapshot

Total industry sales of sporting goods and equipment were $21.4 billion in 2000, up 8.8 percent over 1999 levels of $19.6. While golf is the sport that generates the most revenue in sales of equipment ($3.7 billion), inline skating and other wheel sports including skateboarding and scooters, were the fastest growing in revenues. Retail sales associated with skateboards and scooters were up 127 percent in 2000, to $1 billion from $473 million in 1999. Nearly 80 percent of total industry revenues are from the sale of equipment for these seven categories: golf, exercise, team sports, hunting and firearms, fishing and tackle, camping, and inline skating and other wheel sports.

Purchase Drivers

Sports provide the participant a sense of accomplishment and well-being, health benefits, and stress relief. Sports can become a compelling hobby in which one or all members of the family can participate. Practitioners of various sports have to purchase the right equipment to be a "player"—the right clubs, shoes, clothes, accessories, and so forth. Men, in particular, like competitive sports, including the competitive purchase of sporting accessories. "My husband is really involved in buying sporting goods. It's a luxury and very expensive. Most sports are expensive. But my husband really needs it as an outlet. It's his time with the guys, without the stress of the office. He

CONSUMER SPORTS EQUIPMENT BY SPORT

Sales, in $ millions

	1999	**2000**	**Change**
Golf	$3,567.3	$3,744.2	5.0%
Exercise	3,396.0	3,643.2	7.3
Team goods	2,408.1	2,456.0	2.0
Hunting and firearms	2,436.7	2,256.0	(7.4)
Fishing tackle	1,916.8	2,030.2	5.9
Camping	1,264.8	1,343.5	6.2
In-line and wheel sports	473.3	1,074.4	127.0
Optics	718.0	729.1	1.5
Skiing, alpine	647.7	547.8	(15.4)
Tennis	338.3	378.0	11.7
Billiards, pool	354.1	359.0	1.4
Skin diving and scuba	362.5	355.3	(2.0)
Baseball and softball	329.4	319.0	(3.2)
Basketball	293.4	285.6	(2.7)
Archery	261.8	254.4	(2.8)
Skiing, snowboards	225.6	234.3	3.9
Bowling	159.5	162.3	1.8
Hockey and ice skates	136.6	136.0	(0.4)
Football	84.1	84.9	1.0
Soccer balls	63.9	65.1	1.9
Water skis	51.2	50.2	(2.0)
Racquetball	43.9	42.0	(4.3)
Table tennis	41.1	40.7	(1.0)
Skiing, cross-country	42.2	33.6	(20.4)
Volleyball and badminton sets	30.0	29.3	(2.3)
Total sports equipment	$19,639.0	$21,372.8	8.8

Source: National Sporting Goods Association
Note: Numbers may not add to total due to rounding.

works hard at the hobby. And it gives him health benefits." But what is stress relief for one can be stress inducing for another, "To me sports and exercise is a stress. It means sweating and working hard."

One consumer explains how she and her family cut back on certain discretionary expenses to allow them to pursue their passion for skiing. "We drive old cars, but we get to ski all winter long. It is all about what you and your family think is important. We don't care if people are impressed by the car we drive, but we have a whole ton of fun on the ski slopes. There are tradeoffs. What is one family's idea of fun isn't the same as another's. Some want a pool in the backyard. For us it's the time spent skiing."

Demographic Variables

Men are the primary buyers of sporting goods and equipment in the household. Over half of men (51 percent) report purchasing sporting goods, compared with only 38 percent of women. The purchase of sporting goods skews toward those under age 55. Sporting goods purchases drop off sharply for households aged 55 and older. Middle-to-high-income households, those with incomes of $35,000 and above, purchase more sporting goods. The presence of children in the home is linked to increased purchase incidence, with 56 percent of households with kids purchasing, compared with 36 percent of those without. Higher levels of educational attainment also correspond to higher purchasing incidence of sporting goods.

 KEY DEMOGRAPHICS FOR BUYERS OF SPORTING GOODS

- *Male-led category*
- *Rises with income and education*
- *Youthful skew, households under age 55*
- *Households with children*

WHAT PEOPLE BUY:
Florals and greenery for indoor use

Forty-four percent of households purchased florals and plants for indoor use during 2001, up from 36 percent in 2000.

Industry Snapshot

Total consumer spending on indoor plants, including artificial flowers, was about $3.6 billion in 2000, $2.3 billion of which was spent on artificial flowers, according to the Bureau of Economic Analysis. Americans spent $1.3 billion on indoor plants, as tracked by the National Gardening Association.

Purchase Drivers

Indoor gardening allows the homeowner to bring the outdoors in, decorating the home with plants. Indoor gardening can be as simple as an African Violet on the window sill, or as elaborate as greenhouses and other major layouts equipped with grow lights, hydroponic culture, and special heating systems.

The Lifestyle Market Analyst, 2000 reports that 35 percent of the total adult population are "houseplant enthusiasts." Other interests of these enthusiasts are sewing, needlework/knitting, and health/natural foods. A green thumb for indoor plants also relates to a green thumb outdoors. About 66 percent of houseplant enthusiasts are also interested in flower gardening, and 43 percent are vegetable gardeners.

Demographic Variables

Slightly more women than men report buying florals and greenery for indoor use in 2001, suggesting that this category is a female-led one. The highest purchasing incidence is among those aged 55 to 64, with those aged 45 to 54 just slightly behind in purchasing incidence. Although there is a skew toward more mature consumers, there also is an up-tick in purchase incidence among 25 to 34 year olds.

Florals and indoor greenery are more widely bought by middle-to-upper-income households, those $35,000 and above. Purchase incidence rises with household size, so households with two or more

---

INDOOR PLANTS AND ARTIFICIAL FLOWERS

Sales in $ billions, 2000

Artificial flowers	$2.3
Indoor plants	1.3
Total	3.6

Sources: Bureau of Economic Analysis, National Gardening Association

---

individuals buy more in this category. The presence of children in the home, however, has little impact on purchase incidence.

 KEY DEMOGRAPHICS FOR BUYERS OF FLORALS AND INDOOR GREENERY

- *Female-led*

- *Household income $35,000 and above*

- *Larger households, but no impact from presence of children*

- *Skews toward more mature households, aged 45 and older, but with a slight rise among those aged 25 to 34*

WHAT PEOPLE BUY:
Aromatherapy and scented household products, such as potpourri steamers

Purchase of aromatherapy and scented household products rose slightly in 2001 to 42 percent, up from 39 percent of U.S. households in 2000. Aromatherapy and other scented products often take the place or serve the same function in the home that scented candles do: to enhance the atmosphere of the home with pleasant, emotionally evocative scents.

Industry Snapshot

The home-fragrance market, excluding candles, totaled $1.8 billion in 2000, with just over half of industry sales, or $1 billion, attributed to the category of home-fragrance diffusers. Room sprays totaled $383 million in retail sales, while potpourri reached $213 million. Manufacturer and marketer S.C. Johnson, the private company that markets home-fragrance products under the Glade brand name, is the market-share leader in the home-fragrance category.

Purchase Drivers

Consumers buy aromatherapy and scented household products for much the same reason they buy candles. In describing her purchase of aromatherapy products, one woman told us, "I buy anything scented lilac. It's my favorite scent. I feel good when I walk into my house and it smells like lilac." Scents have powerful effects on consumers' emotions, and more manufacturers are looking at opportunities to enhance the appeal of their products through the addition of aromas.

Demographic Variables

Women lead in purchasing aromatherapy products, with 45 percent of women reporting a purchase, compared with 39 percent of men. This category has a strong youthful skew, with purchase incidence highest among the 25-to-34-year-old households. Purchase incidence is elevated for householders aged 18 to 54, and drops sharply at age 55. Regionally, households in the southern states purchase the most aro-

RETAIL SALES IN HOME-FRAGRANCE MARKET

Sales in $ millions, 2000

	Sales	Market Share
Diffusers	$980.5	53%
Room sprays	383.7	21
Potpourri	213.2	12
Specialty room	170.5	9
Wardrobe	85.3	5
Total	**$1,833.2**	

Sources: Kline & Company, Unity Marketing

matherapy products. Black consumers also exhibit a higher purchase incidence than whites or Hispanics.

There is little variation in the purchase incidence of aromatherapy in terms of household income. Household size and presence of children make a difference, with larger sized households of two or more individuals and those with children purchasing more.

 KEY DEMOGRAPHICS FOR BUYERS OF AROMATHERAPY AND HOME FRAGRANCE

- *Women-led category*
- *Income makes little difference*
- *Households under age 55*
- *Black consumers report higher incidence*
- *Large households and those with children*
- *Southern households*

WHAT PEOPLE BUY:
Pet accessories

Consumers are buying more for their pets, with the purchase incidence of pet accessories rising to 42 percent of U.S. households in 2001 from 35 percent in 2000. In the most recent study done of pet ownership by the American Veterinary Medical Association, nearly 60 percent of U.S. households (58.9 million) owned one or more pets, or companion animals as they are called in the study. American households keep 59 million cats and nearly 53 million dogs. Consumers are more likely to have multiple cats than dogs, so there are 4.2 million more households that own dogs.

Industry Snapshot

Consumer spending on their pets reached $28.5 billion in 2001, according to the American Pet Products Manufacturers Association, rising 24 percent over spending of $23 billion in 1998. Pet-owning households are reported to spend on average $460 each year on their pets.

Purchase Drivers

Today's pet-owning households tend to look at their pets as members of the family, rather than simply animals. A respondent explains, "We have a dog and a cat. They are like members of the family." Pets are often treated as surrogate children, given toys, and taken on play or adventure outings. One consumer explains, "We have four cats, a fish, and a guinea pig. Our cats have to have their toys." Another says, "It took us five years to have a baby. During that time, my pets were my children. If you don't have children, then you put a lot into your pets because they fill that need to care for someone. Then when you have kids, it becomes a money factor, a time factor, and a room factor. My animals suffered a change in living standards."

The American Pet Products Manufacturers Association reports that the majority of pet owners bought a gift for their pet in the past year. Typically, gifts are purchased for either no special occasion or for Christmas.

TOTAL U.S. PET INDUSTRY EXPENDITURES

Retail sales, in $ billions

Year	Sales	% Growth
1998	23.0	—
2001	28.5	24
2002 estimated	29.5	4
2003 projected	31.0	5

Source: American Pet Manufacturers Association

Demographic Variables

Both genders are equally involved in purchasing pet accessories. Buying pet accessories spans a wide age range, with those households under age 55 purchasing more often than those aged 55 and older. White households, as opposed to black and Hispanic households, lavish more spending on accessories for their pets. Purchase incidence of pet accessories is highest among the highest-income households, $50,000 and above. Buying pet accessories is a family affair; households with three or more members and those with children purchase significantly more pet accessories than single-or two-person households.

 KEY DEMOGRAPHICS FOR BUYERS OF PET ACCESSORIES

- *Gender neutral*
- *Rises with income, highest for households with incomes of $50,000 or more*
- *Households under age 55*
- *Larger households and those with children*
- *Highest among white households*

WHAT PEOPLE BUY:
Furniture

Purchase incidence of furniture rose somewhat in 2001, reaching 41 percent of U.S. households, up from 35 percent the prior year. The purchase of furniture can range from inexpensive occasional tables, ready-to-assemble, and unfinished furniture, to major furniture acquisitions that are often bought on credit and paid for over time.

Industry Snapshot

The furniture industry has been undergoing a retrenchment in the past several years. Furniture retailing is evolving, with many large chains of independently owned furniture stores going out of business, while branded furniture companies open dedicated, often franchised gallery stores to assure continued distribution at the consumer level. National specialty chains such as Pier 1 and Bombay Company are also capturing a greater share of the furniture market, offering affordably priced imports manufactured to their specifications. Despite the upheaval at the retail end, personal consumption of furniture reached $64.1 billion in 2000, up 6.8 percent over 1999 levels of $60 billion.

Accounting for a 45 percent share of the market in 2000, wood furniture, called case goods by the industry, is the largest segment of the furniture market and totaled $28.7 billion at retail. Upholstered furniture, with $17.6 billion in sales, is the second-largest category with 27 percent share. Mattresses and box springs, with 13 percent share of market and $8.5 billion in sales, is the third largest category in the furniture market.

Purchase Drivers

While more consumers are turning to decorative accessories to update their room décor, they often buy furniture to replace a worn-out piece. Often thought of as a necessity, one focus group respondent views all furniture purchases as discretionary, "We have all the basics [furniture] that we need. I view all [furniture purchases] as discretionary. I just bought a grandfather clock. It is fun. It is the first thing you see when you walk into the house." After moving to the Midwest from Florida, one respondent needed to change her home décor to

RETAIL FURNITURE SALES

Sales by type, in $ billions, 2000

	2000 Sales	Share of Market
Furniture total	**$64.0**	
Outdoor total	**2.3**	**3.5%**
Porch, lawn, beach, and similar	0.3	
Metal porch, lawn, outdoor	2.0	
Wood total	**28.7**	**44.7**
Unpainted or unassembled.	3.9	
Infant's and children's	0.9	
Bedroom.	8.0	
Living room, library, family room and den	5.2	
Dining room and kitchen, not cabinets	7.9	
Office furniture	0.4	
Household furniture, other	2.3	
Upholstered furniture total	**17.6**	**27.4**
Sofas and other	9.2	
Upholstered wood chairs.	5.9	
Household, other	2.5	
Metal furniture total	**4.8**	**7.4**
Household dining room and kitchen	2.3	
Bed frames, cots, and other beds.	0.7	
Infants' highchairs, carseats, and other.	0.7	
Household furniture, other	0.9	
Mattresses and bedding sets	**8.5**	**13.2**
Innerspring, including cribs and bedsprings. . . .	6.7	
Sleep system ensembles, not waterbeds	0.3	
Dual-purpose sleep furniture.	1.4	
Reed, rattan, fibrous, plastic total	**1.0**	**1.6**
Household furniture, plastic and fibrous.	0.2	
Reed and rattan, including willow, wicker, cane .	0.7	
Other furniture	**1.4**	**2.2**

Source: Bureau of Economic Analysis.
Note: Numbers might not add to totals due to rounding.

be more compatible with the local neighborhood. "We used to live in Florida and had very contemporary furnishings. Then we moved to Ohio, and it didn't have the same feeling. We needed to buy all new furniture to match our new home."

Demographic Variables

Furniture purchases often represent major household expenditures, so that men and women are equally involved in the purchase. Men, in fact, report a higher purchase incidence of furniture (44 percent) than women do (38 percent). Furniture buying tends to skew toward a more youthful market, with households aged 18 to 34 reporting the highest purchase incidence. Furniture purchasing remains elevated through age 54 and then declines sharply among those aged 55 and older.

Purchase incidence is highest among households with incomes of $50,000 and above. Larger households of two or more members and those with children have a higher purchase incidence of furniture than do single-person households and those without children.

 KEY DEMOGRAPHICS FOR BUYERS OF FURNITURE

- *Joint purchases*
- *Rises with income*
- *Skews toward youthful market, drops after age 55*
- *Larger households and those with children*

WHAT PEOPLE BUY:
Crafts, craft supplies, sewing, knitting, and needlework

Consumers are spending more time crafting, sewing, knitting, and doing needlework with their hands, as reflected in purchase incidence, which rose from 33 percent of households in 2000 to 39 percent in 2001. A hobby for some, cheap "therapy" for others, crafting is enjoyed by over half of U.S. households, according to research conducted by the Hobby Industry Association. Susan Brandt, director of communications at the Hobby Industry Association, explains that interest in crafts is on the rise after the 9/11 attacks: "We are an industry people go to in times of trouble. They take solace in staying busy and doing things with their hands."

Industry Snapshot

New research from the Hobby Industry Association puts the hobby industry at $23 billion, with general crafts ($9 billion) and needlecrafts ($8 billion) accounting for about three-fourths of industry sales. Mass merchants and discount chains are the leading retailer of craft accessories, accounting for 25 percent of total industry sales, while dedicated craft chains make up 19 percent of sales. Michaels Stores is the nation's largest specialty craft retailer, with nearly 700 stores in operation. The chain generated $2.2 billion in revenues in 2000, with Michaels predicting sales in 2001 to rise 8 to 10 percent, largely due to sales increases after 9/11. Michaels Stores growth has become legendary, rising from a chain of only 16 stores in the mid-1980s. What accounts for its growth? Keeping focused on its mission—to help people express themselves creatively—the company has found a formula for success that taps deep-seated longings in people everywhere.

Purchase Drivers

Crafting provides a creative outlet that many consumers need, especially in today's complex, technology-driven society. A respondent explained, "If you have a creative nature, you have to do something. For some, it is art, or acting, or writing, but for me it is crafts. I have to have an outlet, something to do with my hands." Crafting relieves

---

CRAFT AND HOBBY INDUSTRY

Retail sales in $ billions, 2000

	2000 Sales	Market Share
General crafts	9.0	39%
Needlecrafts	8.0	35
Painting and finishing	4.0	17
Floral	2.0	9
Total	**23.0**	**100**

Source: Hobby Industry Association

---

stress for some, as another consumer says, "It takes the place of me going to a therapist."

The Hobby Industry Association reports that the five most popular craft activities in descending order are: cross-stitching, 16 percent; home-decor painting, 13 percent; cake decorating, 12 percent; crocheting, 12 percent; and scrapbooking/memory crafts, 11 percent.

Demographic Variables

Crafting is a female-dominated activity with women reporting much higher purchase incidence for their household (43 percent) than men (35 percent). The prime ages for purchasing crafts are from 45 to 54, with purchase incidence among younger consumers rising with age. As with most categories, purchase incidence drops sharply at age 65. Whites participate in craft purchasing more than blacks. Middle-to-upper-income households ($35,000 or more) buy more crafts than do lower-income families. Larger households, especially those with children, buy more craft supplies than do single-person households.

 KEY DEMOGRAPHICS FOR BUYERS OF CRAFT AND HOBBY SUPPLIES

- *Female-oriented market*

- *Incomes of $35,000 or more*

- *Households under age 55, with incidence dropping sharply after age 65*

- *Households with two or more persons and those with children buy more*

WHAT PEOPLE BUY:
Audio equipment, stereo systems, etc.

In 2001, 35 percent of U.S. households reported purchasing audio equipment and stereo systems, up from 31 percent in 2000. This is a category that has seen technological innovations with the migration of sound recording from analog (tapes, vinyl) to digital (CDs). Listening to music, records, tapes, and CDs is an extremely popular lifestyle interest, enjoyed regularly by 52.8 million Americans, according to the *Lifestyle Market Analyst, 2000.*

Industry Snapshot

The sales of home electronics, including audio equipment, were a bright spot in an otherwise dismal Christmas season in 2001. While the numbers for 2001 were not in as this book went to press, the sales of audio equipment reached $18.8 billion in 2000, up 11.1 percent over 1999 levels. Americans, particularly young American men, have an insatiable appetite for the latest technology, and the audio industry has benefited from continuous demand for the latest-and-greatest audio technology systems. The migration to digital has led to investment in new sound systems and the proliferation of surround-sound, home-entertainment systems make yesterday's two-speaker systems totally antiquated. Consumer demand for better and more authentic sound technology will keep this market vibrant in the years to come.

Purchase Drivers

Consumers accent their life with music, using it to set a tone or a mood in the home. As they continue to spend more and more time in their home havens, consumers see a need for high-quality audio equipment to bring the sounds of life into the home. One respondent explains, "My husband has been studying classical music and composers for the last couple of years. While we have a portable CD player, that became less adequate as his interest in music grew. So this year we bought a complete home-entertainment system that has surround sound. It even plays DVDs, so we had to get a new flat-screen television, too, to get the most from the system."

AUDIO EQUIPMENT
Retail sales in $ billions, 2000

	Retail Sales	Change
1998.	$15.4	—
1999.	17.0	10.2%
2000.	18.0	11.1

Source: Bureau of Economic Analysis

Demographic Variables

Men are the prime purchasers of audio sound equipment in the household. In our survey, 41 percent of men reported their households bought such equipment in 2001, compared with only 29 percent of women, suggesting that more men than women are bringing new equipment into the home. This is a youth market, with purchase incidence highest among the youngest households, aged 18 to 24. Purchase incidence remains strong, however, through age 54, when it drops to 20 percent; after age 54 purchase incidence continues to decline with age. Notably, the leading edge of the baby-boom generation has now reached age 55. Will this generation's continued aging signal a declining interest in music? Or will boomers continue to have a steady appetite for music and audio systems?

Black households report higher purchase incidence of audio equipment than do white households. Purchase incidence is highest among middle-to-high-income households, those with incomes of $35,000 or more. The presence of children under age 18 in the home correlates positively with increased purchase incidence of audio equipment. More highly educated households, those with some college or more, also purchase more audio equipment.

 KEY DEMOGRAPHICS FOR BUYERS OF AUDIO EQUIPMENT, STEREO SYSTEMS

- *Male-dominated market*
- *Middle-to-upper income*
- *Black households*
- *Households with children*

- *Younger households, aged 18 to 34; sharp drop after age 55*
- *Higher education, some college or more*

WHAT PEOPLE BUY:
Collectibles

In 2001, 34 percent of households reported buying collectibles, compared with about 31 percent in 2000. The dictionary defines "collectible" as "an object that is collected by fanciers, especially one other than such traditionally collectible items as art, stamps, coins, and antiques." With little guidance provided by the type of object that is considered collectible, the key to the definition of the term is that it is something—anything—that a fancier brings together into one body or place. The more I study the phenomenon of collecting, the less sure I am of what it really is, since collecting is an integral part of our everyday lives, the getting and gathering of things with special meaning to the individual. Even the most disenfranchised members of our society, homeless people, carry "collections" of objects around with them. In some strange way, these objects, whether they are tin cans or just cast-offs from others, connect the street person with the life they led before. It represents some normalcy and a connection with "home" in an otherwise dysfunctional lifestyle. Collecting isn't something that the other guy does. We all do it in some way or another, even if we haven't yet discovered what exactly it is that we collect.

Industry Snapshot

In 2000, collectible retail sales dropped about 6.7 percent from 1999. The industry has suffered from the lack of strong products, which capture the hearts and imagination of the collectors, as Beanie Babies did a few years ago. Without hot new properties, the industry is undergoing a period of adjustment and retrenchment at the beginning of the third millennium.

While the collectibles industry, defined as companies that manufacture and market new products for the express purpose of being collected by adult collectors, is on the downswing, collecting as a consumer passion or hobby has never been more popular. About 42.9 million U.S. households, that is 42 percent of total households, collect. With an average of 1.7 individual collectors living in each collecting household, the total number of U.S. collectors is estimated at 72.9 million, about 35 percent of the total U.S. population.

Not all collectible categories declined. The category of collectible ornaments, as distinguished from "tree-and-trim," increased 6.7 percent to $623.6 million in retail sales; music boxes and musicals were up 1.6 percent to reach $171.7 million; and collectible-type dolls rose 2.2 percent to reach $929.9 million.

Purchase Drivers

With collecting being a rapidly growing hobby, it stands to reason that companies in the collectibles industry should be the prime beneficiaries of this market expansion. However, it appears that many new collectors are collecting items not produced new by collectibles companies. Rather they are pursuing other types of products, including vintage items, available on the secondary market, at auctions, and through internet services like eBay. Consequently, the definition of what is a collectible is beginning to shift from an object that is "fancied" to one that has potential investment value. Today when you say something is "collectible," it implies that someday it may be worth serious money. The emergence of eBay, *Antiques Roadshow,* and other venues that focus on finding treasures in the attic have given rise to this shift in definition.

A major reason why the collectibles industry is not benefiting from the collecting boom is that today's collectors are very different from the traditional target market collectible companies have been marketing to for years. Today's collecting consumers are:

- Younger and have more discretionary income to spend on their collecting passions;

- Empowered consumers who are highly discerning. They will not buy just anything, but demand something very special and unique.

- More highly educated; they know what "limited edition" really means.

Demographic Variables

Men and women report an equal incidence of purchasing collectibles in their households. Collectibles purchasing peaks in two age ranges: among the youngest consumers aged 18 to 24 and for 45-to-54-year-olds. Traditionally, collecting has been a hobby associated with consumers in their empty-nesting years. However, today's younger

COLLECTIBLE SALES BY PRODUCT FORM, 1999–2000

Sales in $ millions

	1999	2000	Change 1999–2000	Market Share
Figurines and sculpture, total	$2,780.0	$2,370.8	(14.7)%	33%
Porcelain	858.2	704.2	(17.9)	10
Cold cast	1,709.3	1,478.8	(13.5)	21
Figurines, other	212.5	187.8	(11.6)	3
Dolls, total	910.1	929.9	2.2	13
Vinyl		232.5		3
Porcelain		567.2		8
Other		130.2		2
Plush toys	1,022.5	752.7	(26.4)	11
Die cast	582.2	562.6	(3.4)	8
Cottages/villages	617.7	568.6	(7.9)	8
Cottages only	200.3	170.2	(15.0)	2
Villages only	417.4	398.4	(4.6)	6
Ornaments	584.3	623.6	6.7	9
Plates	250.4	214.9	(14.2)	3
Boxes/musicals	369.4	366.9	(0.7)	5
Boxes, non-music	200.3	195.2	(2.5)	3
Music boxes	169.0	171.7	(1.6)	2
Steins	125.2	116.6	(6.9)	2
Other	408.7	633.8	55.1	9
Total	**$7,650.5**	**$7,140.4**	**(6.7)**	**100**

Source: Unity Marketing

consumers, particularly young men intrigued with the new capabilities to find desirable collectible items on the internet, are pursuing collecting actively. White households, as opposed to black and Hispanic households, are more likely to buy collectibles.

Buying collectibles is a practice of moderate-income households. Households in the $35,000-to-less-than-$50,000 income range have the highest purchase incidence of collectibles. Household size correlates with collectibles purchase, with households with three or more individuals and those with children more likely to purchase collectibles.

 KEY DEMOGRAPHICS FOR BUYERS OF COLLECTIBLES

- *Gender neutral*
- *Moderate household incomes*

- *Two age segments: 18 to 24 and 45 to 54*
- *White households predominate*
- *Larger households and those with children*

WHAT PEOPLE BUY:
Lamps and lighting accessories

Purchase incidence of lamps and lighting accessories rose from about one-fourth of households in 2000 to one-third in 2001. While lighting is an essential component of everyday life, it also serves a decorative function, with lamps being a key decorative accessory. The effects of lighting are a key element for creating a mood of peacefulness and harmony in the home. People buy lamps and lighting as much for need as desire, making them essential, yet discretionary.

Industry Snapshot

In 2000, the sales of lamps and lighting accessories totaled $3.8 billion, according to statistics compiled by the Bureau of Economic Analysis. Portable residential lighting, or lamps, captured just over half of total sales.

Purchase Drivers

New lamps and lighting can change a room, yet often consumers buy them as part of a more extensive makeover. As seen in other home décor purchases, one purchase—say a new chair or a new rug—made to replace a worn-out item often results in a cascade of additional home purchases justified by the original purchase. Since lamps are by their very nature mechanical, replacing a broken or worn-out lamp can become the driving force behind more extensive household purchases. One respondent's example illustrates this point perfectly: "All our furniture is hand-me-downs, but I needed new lamps for the family room. Then I needed to get new furniture there, too. It was long overdue."

Demographic Variables

Men and women participate equally in the purchase of lamps and lighting accessories for their home. There are two peak ages for the purchase of lamps and lighting: ages 18 to 24, corresponding with the household formation years, and ages 45 to 54. Purchase incidence remains strong during the years between the two peak buying periods, but drops off sharply after age 55.

LAMPS AND LIGHTING ACCESSORIES

Retail sales in $ millions, 2000

	Sales
Portable residential lighting and fixtures	$2,087.2
Residential lighting fixtures	448.5
Incandescent hand, portable lighting equipment	856.0
Lamps and lanterns, non-electric	271.6
Components and parts for lighting equipment	107.2
Total	3,770.6

Source: Bureau of Economic Analysis

With a purchase incidence of 43 percent, black-American households purchased more lamps than white or Hispanic households, at 32 percent and 33 percent respectively. Households with incomes of $50,000 or more report the highest incidence for purchasing lamps and lighting accessories. Households with children under age 18 and those with more individuals also purchase more lamps. There is also a link between college education and the purchase of lamps and lighting. Presumably, these more-educated households read more and therefore purchase more lamps to aid their study.

 KEY DEMOGRAPHICS FOR BUYERS OF LAMPS AND LIGHTING EQUIPMENT

- *Gender neutral*
- *Black households*
- *Rises with income and education; households with incomes of $50,000 or more buy more*
- *Two peaks: ages 18 to 24 and 45 to 54*
- *Larger households and those with children under age 18*

WHAT PEOPLE BUY:
Vases, urns, and pots

Just under one-third of consumers in 2001 purchased a vase, urn, or pot. These accessories are becoming more important as a decor item, offering both decorative values as well as the functional benefit of holding flowers, plants, or other display material.

Industry Snapshot

Vases, urns, and pots are part of the $16.5 billion home decorative segment of the giftware market. Total sales of vases, urns, and pots were just under $1 billion in 2000, rising 21 percent over retail sales in 1998. While vases can be positioned as single decorative accents, many tableware manufacturers produce coordinating vases that match the pattern of their dinnerware, thus making the vase a part of the overall dining experience.

Purchase Drivers

The overall gifts market is strongly affected by the trend toward home. Consumers are spending more money buying decorative accents as the home market shifts from a functional orientation to a fashion business. Today's consumers are enhancing and updating their décor through accessories, adding small accent pieces such as vases, textiles, pillows and rugs, wall décor, and other decorative items. The gifts industry is responding to this market shift, as it presents fashionable home-accent pieces priced right for impulse purchase and gift-giving. Adding to growth in sales of vases and other decorative accents is the new availability of these items at retail. The nation's home furnishing specialty chains, such as Williams-Sonoma, Bed Bath & Beyond, Pier 1, Pottery Barn, Crate&Barrel, Yankee Candle, and Kirklands, are redefining the competitive home-furnishings landscape. They are leaving the traditional furniture stores marginalized as consumers demand more relevant home-shopping experiences and new products that reflect their personal lifestyles.

VASES, URNS, AND POTS

Retail sales in $ millions

	Sales	Change
1998	$790.0	—
1999	1,046.4	32.0%
2000	958.5	(8.3)

Source: Unity Marketing

Demographic Variables

Vases, urns, and pots are a gender-neutral category with only a slightly higher purchasing incidence reported by women. In terms of age, no spikes appear that would mark a prime age-group target for this category. Rather, consumers up through age 65 have about the same purchase incidence for vases. Black households report a higher purchase incidence of vases than do white or Hispanic households, suggesting that black households may have stronger preferences for vases, urns, and pots as a home decorative accent.

The highest-income houses, those making $50,000 or more, have the highest reported purchase incidence of vases. Household composition does not strongly affect the purchase of vases, with two-person households buying substantially more than one-person households, and slightly more than those with three or more members.

 KEY DEMOGRAPHICS FOR BUYERS OF VASES, URNS, AND POTS

- *Gender neutral*
- *Highest-income households buy more*
- *No specific age is prime*
- *Larger households and those with children*
- *Black households choose more often as decoration*

WHAT PEOPLE BUY:
Art, prints, lithographs

Just over one-quarter of U.S. households (27 percent) reported buying art, prints or lithographs in 2001, compared with 21 percent in 2000. Today's consumer market for art is being strongly affected by the availability of ready-to-hang art at retail outlets ranging from mass merchants and discounters to home-specialty stores. No longer are consumers required to seek decorative art in out-of-the-way galleries and art dealers, or pay exorbitant prices to custom frame a print. Ready-framed art, as well as the explosion of specialty framing boutiques that offer affordable and quick frames, have opened the art market to the masses.

The consumer market for art reached a staggering $31.7 billion in sales in 2000, rising 6 percent over the previous year's levels of $29.9 billion. The art market is rapidly becoming a mass market. Pre-framed prints are available at all sorts of outlets, including Wal-Mart, Target, and Kmart, as well as at national, specialty, home-furnishing chains, such as Bed Bath & Beyond, Bombay Company, Pier 1, and Linens 'n Things. In addition, a more clearly differentiated market at the luxury end is emerging for connoisseurs. The fastest-growing category in the art market in 2001 is original art, defined as one-of-a-kind work, such as watercolor, oil painting, pencil sketch, and chalk drawing. Moreover, recent advances in art reproduction technologies, such as printing on canvas and Giclée, appeal most to the upper end of the art buying market. Original art is more available and accessible than ever before to today's art buyer. Art buyers also are more sophisticated and better educated, so they can truly appreciate the value of owning a one-of-a-kind piece.

Purchase Drivers

For some consumers, art is something they put on their walls to match the colors of their sofa. Once the piece is hung, it becomes part of the architecture of the room, like the windows and doors. One focus group respondent told us, "I have kept the same pictures my entire 35 years of marriage, longer than I have kept anything else in my home. I buy something and if it fits, it stays." Others, however, collect

---

TOTAL ART INDUSTRY SALES TO CONSUMERS

Sales 1999–2000, in $ billions

	1999 Sales	1999 Market Share	2000 Sales	2000 Market Share	Change
Art reproductions	$19.2	64%	$18.7	59%	(2)%
Original art	6.5	22	9.1	29	40
Custom framing	4.2	14	3.9	12	(7)
Total	29.9	100	31.7	100	6

Source: Unity Marketing

---

art and use it to create a mood in the home. One respondent who collects art explains, "I appreciate the creativity of the artist. I have both originals and prints. When I go to art shows, I am amazed. It is a real lift to see the art. I enjoy it so much." Another respondent with a passion for mountain lions displays a series of prints in her home: "We have a collection of mountain-lion prints. It is a focal point of our home. When people come into the house, they see our art and find it interesting and want to talk about it."

Art adds decorative value and provides a focal point, but it also colors the emotional mood in the home. As this respondent put it, "Art is like a candle. It makes you feel good. I feel good when there are things hanging in my house that I really like."

Demographic Variables

Art is a gender-neutral category, purchased by men and women at the same rate. Art purchases are slightly elevated among younger consumers aged 18 to 34, with purchase incidence declining slightly after age 35. As in so many other categories, purchase incidence tanks after age 65. Art-purchasing households tend to have higher incomes, with those households making $50,000 or more per year reporting the highest purchase incidence. Household composition has little impact on the purchase of art, with two-person, three-person, and those with children purchasing at about the same rate.

Contributing to the growth in the art market is an increasingly educated consumer market. This also correlates strongly with increased household income levels. With 28 percent of adult Americans older than age 25 having completed four or more years of college, up from 24 percent in 1990, the prospects for the art market look bright for the years ahead. Purchase incidence rises with education, and households with completed college degrees and those with higher levels of educational attainment have the highest purchase incidence.

 KEY DEMOGRAPHICS FOR BUYERS OF ART, PRINTS, AND LITHOGRAPHS

- *Gender neutral*
- *Rises with income and education*
- *Skews toward ages 18 to 34*
- *Household composition is not a factor*

WHAT PEOPLE BUY:
Tabletop china, crystal, silver, sterling flatware, and other dinnerware

Just over one-fourth of households (26 percent) bought tabletop china, crystal, sterling flatware, or other dinnerware in 2001. That represents a significant jump from the 16 percent of households that reported the same in 2000. Contributing to the increase in purchase incidence in the category is a new emphasis on the home and home entertaining. In addition, more consumers are expanding their selection of dinnerware from everyday and special-occasion, by buying alternative dinnerware patterns to match the season, holiday, or special mood of the occasion. Home-decorating mavens, notably Martha Stewart, have promoted the trend by exposing consumers to new unconventional ideas about home decorating and entertaining and by teaching them how to pull off more sophisticated table settings and displays.

Industry Snapshot

The retail sales of tabletop dinnerware, including china and other dinnerware, glassware, flatware (including sterling sliver and crystal), totaled $6.5 billion in 2000. Retail sales in the category rose 3 percent over sales of $6.3 billion in 1999. The sale of tabletop giftware, including serving pieces, candlesticks, vases, and other coordinating pieces, adds an additional $1.3 billion to the industry's total sales.

The tabletop industry is finding new outlets for its products as consumers turn to the national specialty home-furnishing chains for tabletop and dinnerware. Crate&Barrel, Williams-Sonoma, and Pottery Barn rank among the top-25 tabletop retailers nationwide. Department stores continue their strong hold on the bridal market, but specialty stores are also joining the game, as many, such as Pier 1, have already instituted bridal registries within their stores. At mass-market retailers, Martha Stewart's Everyday at Kmart and Michael Grave's work with Target are attracting a new clientele for tabletop.

Purchase Drivers

The market for tabletop, particularly what is called the "upstairs" market for fine china, crystal, and sterling, has been traditionally associated with the bridal market. Each year 2.2 to 2.5 million Americans get married. As a result, the bridal market for tabletop has been stable since 1970. With tabletop manufacturers primarily focused on department stores as a retail outlet for their bridal business, the continued decline in department stores as a retailing force is likely to have a negative impact on the tabletop industry as well. Today's brides are turning to specialty retailers offering patterns and styles that match better with their more casual lifestyles. One young married woman said, "I have a lot of stuff I got as wedding gifts. All it does is sit in the china cabinet and gather dust. It looks nice, but with the kids, I find we use paper plates when we have parties."

After age 35 or so, women often return to the tabletop market to replace their original bridal patterns with styles more suited to who they have become. One table devotee put it this way, "Tabletop is all about your stage in life. I have had china ever since we were married, but it doesn't fit me anymore. I only use it at Christmas. I love to set a nice table, but I prefer something different today." A passion for tabletop may strike more mature consumers as they venture back into the market to find new styles. "Tabletop is my passion. I love good crystal and setting a really nice table. I have four different china patterns that I use on different occasions. Tabletop is my hobby."

Demographic Variables

The purchase of tabletop china, dinnerware, crystal, and sterling is usually a joint decision, with men and women reporting a nearly equal purchase incidence in the past year. The market for tabletop tends to skew younger, with consumers aged 18 to 44 having the highest reported purchase incidence. Purchase incidence of tabletop drops sharply after age 65. Black-American households report more tabletop purchasing than white or Hispanic households, suggesting that the rising affluence of black Americans is translating into a desire for finer tabletop pieces.

Household income does not seem to be a significant factor, with even lower-income households reporting the purchase of tabletop in 2001. Household size and composition link to tabletop purchase inci-

---

TABLETOP INDUSTRY BY CATEGORY

Sales 1999-2000, in $ billions

	1999	**2000**	**Change**
Dinnerware	$2.5	$2.6	3%
Glassware	1.5	1.6	3
Flatware	1.3	1.2	(2)
Crystal	1.0	1.1	10
Total	6.3	6.5	3

Sources: U.S. Department of Commerce, Retail Census, and Unity Marketing

---

dence with larger households of three or more individuals and those with children buying more.

 KEY DEMOGRAPHICS FOR BUYERS OF TABLETOP CHINA, CRYSTAL, FLATWARE AND DINNERWARE

- *Gender neutral*
- *Income is not a significant factor*
- *Households aged 18 to 44*
- *Larger households and those with children buy more*
- *Strong incidence in black households*

WHAT PEOPLE BUY:
Wall décor, such as sconces, mirrors, tapestries

Consumers have two main choices of how to decorate their walls: either they display art or they use other types of wall décor, including sconces, mirrors, and tapestries. One-fourth of American households purchased wall décor in 2001, just slightly ahead of the 22 percent that purchased from this category in 2000.

Industry Snapshot

The retail sales of wall décor, including sconces, mirrors, and mirror and picture frames, totaled $5.5 billion in 2000. Wall décor has traditionally been more widely distributed than art, which was sold through galleries and framing stores. The emergence of national specialty home-furnishings chains, such as Pottery Barn, Restoration Hardware, Williams-Sonoma, Pier 1, Bed Bath & Beyond, and Linens 'n Things, has opened the market for wall décor to a much broader consumer market.

Purchase Drivers

Blank walls beg to be decorated. That is the main reason that consumers purchase wall décor. The ready availability of more fashion-forward designs has opened new possibilities for wall decoration. Mirrors are always popular, but new designs that feature mirrors with shelves offer decorating and display possibilities for vases, statues, and figurines. Wall sconces are a popular decorative item to use with candles, offering lighting possibilities beyond the tabletop.

Demographic Variables

Wall décor is a gender-neutral category, with men and women reporting an equal purchase incidence. The market for wall décor is more youthful, with the youngest consumers, aged 18 to 24, reporting the highest purchase incidence of wall décor. Purchase incidence declines with advancing age, suggesting that this decorative category has its strongest appeal to the young who are setting up new homes. Black Americans report purchasing more wall décor than whites or Hispanics. The highest-income households buy more wall décor, but

---

WALL DÉCOR, SCONCES, MIRRORS, TAPESTRIES

Retail sales in $ billions, 2000

	Sales
Wall décor	$1.2
Mirror and picture frames	3.3
Mirrors	1.1
Total	5.5

Sources: Bureau of Economic Analysis, Unity Marketing

---

their increased purchase incidence is not particularly pronounced. Larger households and those with children buy more wall décor than do those living in a single-person home.

 KEY DEMOGRAPHICS FOR BUYERS OF WALL DECOR, SCONCES, MIRRORS, AND TAPESTRIES

- *Gender neutral*
- *Black households have higher purchase incidence*
- *Households aged 18 to 24*
- *Larger households and those with children buy more*

WHAT PEOPLE BUY:
Figurines and sculptures

About one-fifth of households reported buying a figurine or sculpture in 2001, about the same as in 2000. A popular gift item, figurines often carry a greeting or social expression that makes them perfect as a gift or remembrance. Figurines are also popular collectibles, with lines, such as Precious Moments and Hummel, passed from generation to generation.

Industry Snapshot

Figurines are the largest category within the contemporary, or manufactured, collectibles market. During the 1990s, figurines captured the popular imagination, especially figurines that carried a social expression greeting or message. However, the last several years have seen the fortunes of the figurine manufacturers and retailers drop as consumers turned to other product categories for gift occasions. In 2000, the figurine segment of the collectibles market totaled $2.4 billion, down nearly 15 percent from 1999 levels of $2.8 billion. Two different kinds of products dominate the figurine market today. Porcelain figurines, which are crafted from porcelain and fired in ovens, account for about 30 percent of the figurine market. Porcelain figurines tend to be more expensive and purchased in stores that deal in high-end merchandise. Cold-cast figurines, so named because they are made of material that cures without firing in an oven, make up nearly two-thirds of the total market. Cold-cast figurines tend to be less costly and widely available at many different types of stores.

Purchase Drivers

Figurines have long been a popular gift and collectible item. The figurines tend to portray characters, people, or animals involved in some universal aspect of life to which many people can relate. Teddy bears have become popular characters for figurines and can be portrayed in a number of ways—usually personified. Popular figurine lines usually carry occasion-based images to cover such events as birthdays, graduations, or first communion. One collector explains, "I collect Precious Moments. I don't collect them all. I look for special ones that

---

FIGURINES AND SCULPTURE

Retail sales in $ billions

	1999	**2000**	**Change**
Figurines and sculpture	$2.8	$2.4	(14.7)
Figurines, porcelain	0.9	0.7	(17.9)
Figurines, cold cast	1.7	1.5	(13.5)
Figurines, other	0.2	0.2	(11.6)

Source: Unity Marketing

say something to me, or that fit an occasion, like a wedding or a gift. If I see the right one, if it means something to me, then I buy it." This collector purchases just one line of figurines, Precious Moments, the teardrop-eyed children created by Sam Butcher that carry an inspirational message. Other consumers may ignore the brand or the product line and select figurines by theme. Thematic-oriented collectors may buy teddy-bear figurines, golf images, clowns, realistic wildlife, or whatever their passion without a second thought to the brand. Another collector explains, "I have an angel collection. It was started by my staff at work, but now I buy angels for me. I have a shelf devoted to my angels in the living room. Everyone knows I love angels so they usually pick that as a gift, but I also buy nice ones I see, especially Victorian-styled angels."

Demographic Variables

Men and women tend to report the same incidence of figurine purchases in their household. Figurine purchasing spans all ages, with the exception of householders older than age 65. The middle-income households, those making $35,000 to less than $50,000, have the highest purchase incidence of figurines. Neither household size nor presence of children in the home links to the purchase of figurines.

KEY DEMOGRAPHICS FOR BUYERS OF FIGURINES AND SCULPTURE

- *Gender neutral*
- *Middle-income households, $35,000 to $50,000*
- *All ages, except 65 and older*

Chapter 6

TRENDS THAT IMPACT WHY PEOPLE BUY THINGS THEY DON'T NEED

What does the future hold for companies in the business of manufacturing, marketing, and selling discretionary products—those things that people desire but don't need? How can these new insights about why people buy things they don't need help companies selling the 30 product categories analyzed in Chapter 5 sell more of their products? How can companies divine the future for the sales of discretionary products and develop plans for action that will increase sales and build market share?

KEY TRENDS SHAPING THE FUTURE OF THE CONSUMER MARKET

Tracking trends is one method many businesses use to foresee the future. Futurists, people who predict trends for businesses, make good copy in the media or guests on television shows as they weave a tale of what the future will look like. Who isn't fascinated when Faith Popcorn presents her vision of the evolving future coined in catchy names and phrases?

I am no futurist, but my company, Unity Marketing, does help our clients see what the future holds for their companies and how to maximize the opportunities that are just over the horizon. We use the same tools most futurists use—wide-ranging environmental scanning, including print and electronic media scans, continuous qualitative and quantitative market research, and ongoing dialogue with key business leaders. However, the results are often different and more specific to the client's business because we focus exclusively on consumer

HOUSEHOLD PROJECTIONS

by age, 2000-2010 (in millions)

	2000	**2005**	**2010**	**% change 2000–2010**
Total	104.1	108.9	114.8	10.3%
Under age 25	5.9	5.4	5.7	-3.4
25–34	18.8	15.6	17.5	-6.9
35–44	24.0	22.6	20.5	-14.2
45–54	20.2	23.9	26.3	25.2
55–64	13.6	17.3	20.7	52.2
65 and older	21.6	23.1	25.1	16.2

Source: U.S. Bureau of the Census

behavior and psychology in the context of industries that market discretionary products.

Here are the key trends we are sharing with our clients today about what the future holds for their businesses. First, we will look at three demographic shifts in the population that are setting the stage for the continued evolution of the consuming trends on the horizon. These trends were developing throughout the consumer psyche long before 9/11, but that terrible, life-changing event has in many ways accelerated the rate of change. It has made these trends a more prominent and more potent force in the U.S. economy.

DEMOGRAPHIC SHIFT | Aging population

Today the gigantic baby-boom generation, roughly 76 million strong, is slowly advancing through its middle age and into maturity. In 2002, the vanguard of the boomer generation, born in 1946, reached age 56 while the trailing-edge boomers, born in 1964, celebrated their 38th birthdays. In the year 2011, the boomer vanguard will slip beyond age 65, marking the entrance into their senior years. By 2029, the entire baby-boom generation will officially be "seniors." The boomer generation has had a profound influence on every socioeconomic and political trend they have touched, usually due to sheer numbers alone. In our democratic culture, a generation of that many people is bound to have a significant impact on everything it touches. As they age into their senior years, the boomers' influence will continue to be felt in strong and lasting ways.

HOUSEHOLD CHARACTERISTICS

	Average Income	Average Household size	Average Number of Children	Average Number of Earners	Home-owners	Some College
Total	$43,051	2.5	0.7	1.3	65%	55%
Under 25	18,276	1.8	0.4	1.3	13	64
25–34	42,470	2.9	1.1	1.5	45	60
45–44	53,579	3.2	1.3	1.7	67	59
45–54	59,822	2.7	0.6	1.8	77	82
55–64	49,436	2.2	0.2	1.3	80	50
65 and older	28,581	1.7	0.1	0.4	80	38

Source: U.S. Bureau of the Census

In the next decade, the total number of U.S. households will grow by 10.3 percent, from 104.1 million in 2000 to 114.8 million in 2010. Due to the aging of the boomers, over that period the number of younger households headed by someone under age 45 will decline while the number of older households will continue to expand. The next generation with the comparable size and thus potential to impact the culture as strongly as the boomers is the boomers' children, called the millennial generation, between 1977 and 1994.

The two fastest-growing household age segments will be aged 55 to 64 (52.2 percent growth) and 45 to 54 (26.2 percent). In most of the 30 discretionary-product categories examined in Chapter Five, we observed a marked change in consumer purchasing behavior starting at about age 55 and well established by age 65. This dramatic change in spending, combined with growth in the number of mature households, signals shifts in demand for most discretionary products.

Today, marketers who are planning for the future need to assess the impact of the aging population on their marketplace. Each company should understand how the aging of the population will affect spending behavior. When today's 35-to-44-year-olds reach age 45 to 54, will they behave the same as they did when they were younger or more like 45-to-54-year-olds preceding them? The answer to these questions will have profound implications for discretionary product marketers, because consumer purchases of discretionary products starts to slow after age 55 and drop sharply at age 65.

KEY DEMOGRAPHICS RELATED TO AGING

Highest income: Households aged 45 to 54 have the highest average income, $59,822, followed by those aged 35 to 44, $53,579.

Largest households: Aged 35 to 44, have 3.2 individuals on average.

Largest number of children: Households aged 35 to 44 have the largest number of children at 1.3, followed closely by those aged 25 to 34.

Most earners: Households aged 45 to 54 have the highest number of individual wage earners (1.8), followed closely by those aged 35 to 44 (1.7), and those aged 25 to 34 (1.5).

Homeownership rises with age: Households headed by persons aged 45 and older report the highest percentage of homeownership.

More-educated: Only 38 percent of Americans older than age 65 have completed at least some college, compared with 62 percent of those older than 45 to 54. The most highly educated age group in our society is those under 25, where 64 percent have at least some college.

FUTURE TRENDS

We foresee that the home will continue to capture more of the household budget in the next ten years. Spending on food and apparel as a percentage of household budget will drop in total share.

Spending on health care, and other health-related expenditures, such as vitamin and nutritional supplements, exercise equipment, spas, and other body "upkeep" services will take a higher percentage of budget as the population ages. Many of these health-related expenditures will be discretionary in nature, purchased to enhance the quality of life, not necessarily because the expenditure is clinically prescribed.

Finally, gift expenditures to others outside the home may well continue to decline as a share of overall spending. There is a reason why the baby-boom generation has also been called the "Me" generation. Gifts are selfless and for another person, and that just does not fit with the basic self-directed focus of the baby-boom generation. Gift giving

---

BEST MARKET FOR DISCRETIONARY PRODUCTS

- Consumer households aged 35 to 44 spend slightly less on household furnishings, $1,590 on average).

- A greater percentage of their total spending is for housing (33.2 percent) and food (14.3 percent), because they have more family members.

- Households aged 45 to 54 have the highest income; spend the most in general; spend the most in the household furnishings and equipment categories ($1,980 on average); and spend the most on gifts to others outside the household ($1,690).

- Consumer households aged 55 to 64 have the third highest average income ($49,436). Their spending on household furnishings ($1,779) and gifts ($1,537) is exceeded only by the 45 to 54 age group.

Source: Bureau of Labor Statistics, CEX

---

will never go away, but boomers fundamentally will be far more involved in buying gifts for themselves than they will be in buying them for others.

DEMOGRAPHIC SHIFT | Rising education level

The average educational level of American consumers is on the rise, and our government's continued emphasis on public education foreshadows a continuation of this trend. Younger people in particular are far more highly educated than the older population. The most highly educated age group in our society is those under age 25, where 64 percent have "some college" or more educational attainment. Many consumer marketers have largely overlooked the potential impact of this key demographic shift. Linked to income levels, educational attainment plays a larger role in consumer behavior than many marketers recognize.

More-educated consumers have very different needs and expectations of the products they buy and the brands they support than less-educated consumers do. More-educated consumers come equipped with a more highly developed and complex set of consuming values, and they know how to research and evaluate information to guide their decision-making. Remember the *tsunami* impact that Ralph

---

HOUSEHOLD SPENDING TRENDS 1990 TO 1999

- In 1999, the percentage spending of the household budget on both food and apparel is down from 1990.

- Percentage spending on transportation, health care, entertainment, personal care, and reading is about the same.

- Percentage spending on housing overall is up, from 30.7 percent of consumer budget in 1990 to 32.6 percent in 2000.

- Household furnishings and equipment, in the home category, rose from 4.0 percent in 1990 to 4.1 percent in 1999. The segments aged 45 to 54 and 55 to 64 posted the highest percentage income growth and spending in this category.

- Spending on gifts to those outside the household is down from 3.2 percent in 1990 to 2.9 percent in 1999. The biggest loss in gift spending was among the group aged 45 to 54, from 4.8 percent of the household budget in 1990 to 3.6 percent in 1999.

Nader and his book *Unsafe at Any Speed* had on the U.S. car industry? He single-handedly had more to do with the shaping of the modern cars we drive than any other individual, company, or industry leader. Think what might happen to any consumer industry if a 21st century "Ralph Nader" examined its product safety, the welfare of its workers, its contribution to society, its protection of the environment, or even support of governments or regimes that support terrorist organizations. A more-educated consumer population may well present new challenges, especially for companies and industries that may not be as "politically correct" as others. Companies can no longer afford to sidestep the safety of their products or react defensively if some product has a flaw or fails completely. Consumers today are just too smart. At the same time, they are more informed and educated in how to manage risks, and they are far more security conscious. Abraham Lincoln said, "You can fool all the people some of the time, and some all of the time, but you cannot fool all the people all the time." Today, with the rising educational levels of the population, it is getting harder and harder to fool them at all.

A more highly educated consumer market represents a challenge to some companies, but for others, it brings wonderful new opportuni-

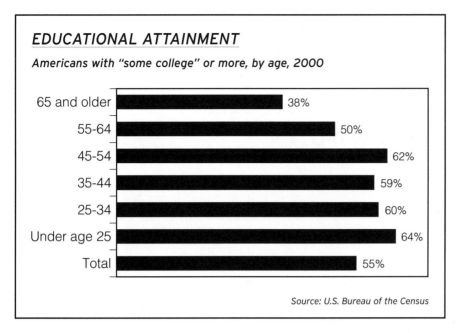

EDUCATIONAL ATTAINMENT

Americans with "some college" or more, by age, 2000

Age	Percent
65 and older	38%
55-64	50%
45-54	62%
35-44	59%
25-34	60%
Under age 25	64%
Total	55%

Source: U.S. Bureau of the Census

ties. Branding is all about establishing an emotional connection between the product or brand and the consumer. You can communicate with a more-educated consumer on a deeper, conceptual level. More-sophisticated, better-educated consumers are receptive to complex branding messages. They have the intellectual tools to absorb such messages and internalize them. In fact, more-educated consumers demand information about their favorite products, companies, and brands. They need information to make their consuming decisions.

In certain categories such as computers, art, and books, educational level is linked to increased purchase incidence. Marketers of these products can anticipate a prosperous future, as a growing market of sophisticated, educationally enhanced consumers demands more of these products. Look at how a company like Gateway has taken the opportunity to sell to better-educated customers through a campaign that uses humor and irony.

DEMOGRAPHIC SHIFT | Minority majority

In California, non-Hispanic whites are already a minority. Within the next 60 years, that will be true throughout the United States. White Americans of non-Hispanic origin will fall below 50 percent of the population, while Hispanics, blacks, and other ethnic groups together

Getting It Right

GATEWAY COMPUTER
Subtle irony sells computers

Frank Purdue said, "It takes a tough man to make a tender chicken." Ted Waitt, CEO of Gateway Computers, is proving it takes a "smart" cow to tell a "dumb" man how to sell computers.

Any high-tech CEO who lets himself play straight man to a talking cow is super-smart in my book. Using irony in product marketing messages has been a big "no-no," because it takes a sophisticated audience to be able to understand it and see through it. However, Waitt and the smart, talking cow reinterpret the dynamics of the Bugs Bunny-Elmer Fudd relationship, and in doing so work marvelously together in communicating their marketing message about the latest and greatest computer gadgetry from Gateway. This series of ads talks to Gateway's sophisticated, educated, entertainment-literate audience.

will represent the national majority. Called the "minority majority" trend, it will bring big changes to our country's cultural, political, economic, and consumer landscape.

While we do not brand one culture bad and another one good, we recognize that people from different cultures behave differently. With America being the melting pot of the world, ethnic stereotypes are part of our cultural mythology. Anglos are reserved, Scots are frugal, French are romantic, Italians are demonstrative, Germans are stubborn, and so forth. The foundations of those ethnic stereotypes are the shared cultural values, expectations, and behavior patterns that children absorb as they grow up in a culture. While emotions are universal and cross all cultural divides, the ways people from different cultures express those emotions differ. Since people make discretionary purchases for emotional reasons, we need to understand how people with different cultural origins express those emotions as consumers. It is in these differences that opportunities and challenges will abound for discretionary marketers in America over the next 60 or so years. In our examination of consumers' purchasing behavior, we found some, but not a lot of differences based upon ethnic heritage.

It is so humbling and so refreshing to see Waitt let the cow be the smart guy and such a wonderful counterpoint to his high-tech CEO cohorts. I personally cannot see Bill Gates or Michael Dell playing second fiddle to a cow, but I would like them more if they did.

What these ads say to me as a consumer is that Gateway is really, truly a different computer company. If Ted Waitt can take directions from the cow, then I, techno-illiterate that I am, can go to the Gateway store and get good direction and advice. I do not need to know anything about computers to buy a Gateway. The cow knows, and that is all that matters. Brilliant, brilliant marketing!

For example, black Americans place a higher priority on education than non-Hispanic whites do as a justifier for discretionary purchases, and they also purchase TVs and other electronic equipment at a higher rate. While few ethnic distinctions were uncovered in this research, we expect more differences in ethnic consumer behavior to be expressed in the next half-century as the "minority majority" trend expands.

The discretionary product categories that are highly tradition bound, such as Christmas and seasonal decorations, home décor, housewares, and tabletop, are expected to be the most affected by the minority majority trend. The whole business of tabletop dinnerware, for example, is predicted to be strongly influenced by the rise of the Hispanic population and their different culturally based needs and expectations for dinnerware and tableware. Just like every culture has its unique cuisine, every culture has its own way of dining, setting the table, serving, and participating in the meal. Today's tabletop industry, especially its marketers of fine china, traces its heritage to 18th and 19th century upper-crust England, and it clings to that heritage

POPULATION PROJECTIONS, 2000-2050

Percent of population by Hispanic and non-Hispanic origin

	Hispanic	Non-Hispanic White	Non-Hispanic Black	Non-Hispanic Other
2000	11.8%	71.4%	11.2%	4.6%
2010	14.6	67.3	12.5	5.6
2020	17.0	63.8	12.8	6.5
2030	19.4	60.1	13.0	7.5
2040	21.9	56.3	13.1	8.6
2050	24.3	52.8	13.2	9.7

Source: U.S. Census Bureau, Population Reports, May 2000

even today. But how many contemporary American consumers aspire to dining as 19th century English landed gentry did?

There is a great opportunity for tabletop and housewares companies to market to the growing ethnically diverse America. However, they need to research and understand each culture's unique dining heritage in order to market contemporary products that reflect that heritage. There is a strong risk for established tabletop companies that they will fall by the wayside if they do not figure out how to bridge the cultural divide and reach out to the emerging minority majority consumers.

CONSUMER TRENDS

Having explored the cultural shifts that are giving rise to the trends, here are the major trends on the horizon that will have the strongest impact on discretionary product manufacturers.

CONSUMER TREND | Shift from buying things to buying experiences

Part of our popular cultural mythology says that when people reach middle age they undergo a personal identity crisis, the "mid-life crisis," that often is played out in the consumer marketplace. Stereotypically, a man may address his mid-life crisis by buying a little red sports car, or more sinisterly, trading in his middle-aged wife for a new, younger model. A woman may get a facelift, dye her hair, find a younger man, or empowered by "menopausal zest," find new energy to pursue a career or hobby. When grandchildren come along, the new grandparents may shower presents and gifts on their grandchildren to make up for some of the inadequacies that their children may have faced when they were growing up because money was tighter. This is the life stage that the boomer generation is now approaching en masse, and it will change the fortunes of many companies that sell and market to people who buy things they don't need.

In their middle years, the members of the baby-boom generation will face the inevitability of their mortality. In doing so, they will try to make up for lost time and the things they may have missed, by directing their energy and money toward experiences and away from the continued acquisition of material things. With the attitude of "been there, done that" in buying more things, boomers will turn away from a consuming focus on things to a hunger for experiences and personal development. Service industries that satisfy the mature boomer's craving for personal enhancement will fare well after 2010. These include travel providers, especially adventure travel modified for aging boomers' health and fitness levels; health and beauty spas; and colleges and adult-education experiences, including training such as cooking or language schools. Consumers will turn away from a focus on the thing consumed (i.e., the noun) to the experience (i.e. the verb).

As boomers pursue new experiential passions, they will need tools, equipment, and accessories to support them in their new pursuits. Discretionary product providers can position themselves for success by providing new products to enhance boomers' experiences and adventures. Durable-goods providers such as automobile manufacturers will fill such a need as will those who manufacture and market sporting goods, personal-care items, books, housewares, and entertainment. For example, boomers will need new recreational vehicles to take them on their new adventures. I predict they will eschew the big, bulky, luxurious RV models so admired by today's mature generation. Instead, they will favor more simplified, environmentally friendly models that can take them off the highway. Think modified VW bus concept crossed with an SUV, equipped with bed, kitchen, and bath, with a powerful engine and 4-wheel drive.

The future focus in consumer behavior will be about buying the experience, so manufacturers and marketers must think beyond the features and benefits of the product they are selling, to how that product supports or enhances an experience. If you came of age in the 1960s as I did, you will remember the strong anti-materialism ethic

QUARTERLY RETAIL AND E-COMMERCE

Sales in $ billions, 1999–2001 (3Q)

	Retail Sales	**Total E-Commerce**	**E-Commerce**
Total 1999	$2,868.0	$15.0	0.5%
Total 2000	3,082.8	27.3	0.9
1st Q 2001	728.7	7.6	1.0
2nd Q 2001	807.4	7.5	0.9
3rd Q 2001	786.6	7.5	1.0

Source: Department of Commerce, U.S. Census Bureau

running through the youth culture. At the same time, 1960s youth hungered after new, mind-opening experiences. Some members of the boomer generation self-destructively turned to sex, drugs, and rock 'n' roll to fulfill much of this craving for experience. I sincerely hope that boomers learned from their youthful excesses, as I foresee that they will participate in a second adolescence in their senior years.

With a "been there, done that" attitude, some boomers will turn away from the pursuit of materialism and excessive consumption and save their money for adventures. New and exciting experiences in their second adolescence could include climbing Mount Everest or at least trekking to base camp. They might decide to travel to China, hike the Appalachian Trail, learn to cook in Paris, or get an advanced degree in English literature. Some may take up painting or photography; set off cross country on a Harley; or learn to fly, sky dive, or balloon. Closer to home, others may take up a second language, join a theater group, form a "garage" band, or, like me, take piano lessons after 30-odd years without touching a keyboard.

Oh, did I mention that I had to buy a piano to play so I could take those piano lessons? Pretty soon, I will be ready to buy the baby grand I really wanted, but felt was a little too extravagant before I knew whether I could recover my piano-playing skills. The Steinway Company and my music store will be thrilled.

CONSUMER TREND | Consumers will crave reality

Our society is undergoing a digital revolution. More of the equipment we interact with daily, from our office computers, cellular phones, microwave ovens, digital televisions, entertainment systems, radios, and even our cars, are digitized and virtually unknowable to ordinary human beings. Where one might have conceptually understood how an analog telephone, television set, or pre-computerized car operated, today you need a degree in computer science or electrical engineering to even begin to comprehend how digital models work. Operating many of these machines presents a challenge to the techno-illiterates. I cannot set the timer on my microwave oven or program the VCR to tape a show without getting out the manuals, but luckily, I have two sons who can do those things for me.

The internet is playing a bigger role in our lives. School children today learn about computers right along with their lessons in reading, writing, and arithmetic. They are exposed to the internet too, with 95 percent of U.S. schools having internet access in 1999, according to the U.S. Center for Education Statistics. Internet use is rising dramatically across the entire population, with the average number of hours spent per person per year on the internet rising from 74 hours in 1998 to 122 hours in 2000, a 65 percent increase. In 2000, roughly 43 percent of the adult population used the internet in the past 30 days, according to a survey reported by Mediamark Research. The internet is also playing an increased role in the commercial side of consumers' lives. In 2000, roughly $27 billion in sales were conducted over the internet. While this is just slightly less than 1 percent of total retail sales of $3.1 trillion, it is a significant contribution to the overall economy.

As our contemporary American society becomes more "virtual," with consumers turning to computers and the internet in their work, for social interaction, entertainment, and shopping, there will be a swing back to the "real" world. Consumers will crave reality. We live and will always live in a real world bounded by time and space and governed by the physical laws of the universe. As our world goes more cyber, consumers will feel the need to surround themselves with things that will bring them back to reality. This will manifest itself in many different areas of our lives, from how we dress, to how we decorate our homes, how we play, and how we entertain ourselves.

As we turn away from buying things and focus more of our spending on experiences, nature travel and history travel will grow. What connects us with the real world more than nature? What grounds us in our cultural reality better than history? History travel, especially travel focused on Civil War sites, is already a booming business and destined to grow. History travel will encompass colonial America, Revolutionary War sites, western expansion, and native cultural attractions as well. Foreign travel will take consumers overseas to the homelands where their ancestors originated.

Grounding through nature will express itself in the garden. Outdoor living space will grow, with consumers building elaborate garden getaways where they can shut out the modern world and enjoy the sounds, smells, and sights of nature. We will invite wildlife into our garden worlds, including birds, but hardly limited to them. We will populate our gardens with turtles, frogs, toads, peaceful snakes, squirrels, bats, even other furry mammals that will connect us better to the real world. A flock of wild turkeys roams our neighborhood. Cars stop on the road just to watch them. They are ugly creatures, looking like miniature "Jurrasic Park" raptors with feathers, but fascinating nonetheless when they come to forage in our yard. I keep food on hand to throw out to them because they seem so special in a First-Thanksgiving, Plymouth-Colony sort of way.

With an emphasis on reality, our home decorating focus will expand to include all five senses. While color and style (i.e., sight) may always dominate our home decor, consumers are broadening their focus to texture (i.e., touch), background music or sounds of running water in indoor fountains (i.e., sound), and home fragrances (i.e., smell). The sense of taste is indulged in our kitchens, now the center and focus of the home.

As we arouse and stimulate our senses through the things with which we surround ourselves, we will pay particular attention to the feel of fabrics in our upholstered furniture, rugs, pillows, throws, bed linens, curtains, towels, and kitchen and dining linens. Shoppers have always been "touchy-feely" when buying these products, but in the future they will become even more so. Consumers will demand that the fabrics they touch, sit on, and cover up with, engage them and stimulate them textually, as well as be a pleasing color and design.

Our taste in home furnishings, including the colors we use to decorate and the art we choose for our walls, will also become more harmonious with nature, more soothing, more natural, and more beautiful. Our taste in color will not fade into pastel nothingness. Rather, we will look for stronger, bolder colors that appear in nature. Think of the bright, bold colors found in a spring garden filled with tulips, daffodils and other flowers. Moreover, we will combine colors not to contrast, but to complement. Art will turn from modern influences with its stress on shapes and colors back to more beautiful, naturalistic images. The continued popularity of the Impressionist painters foreshadows the new direction for art in the third millennium.

In the home of the future, sound will play a more central role. Music that is created to stimulate a mood or a feeling will grow in demand, as consumers enhance their home with new entertainment systems that give the effect of surround sound. Designers will figure out ways to bring the sounds of nature into our homes from simple tabletop fountains that recycle tap water to other more complex fountain designs. Expect architectural design to incorporate a Spanish influence by introducing inner courtyards with natural fountains. Silence itself may become a new luxury and status symbol, with architects incorporating more sound-blocking features in new homes.

Home fragrance will become an essential element of the home. While candles are the preferred means for home-fragrance delivery today, new more flexible mechanisms, such as heated waxes, potpourri boilers, and misters will give consumers more control of the fragrance and the mood the fragrances are intended to set. Aromatherapy technology will be applied to home fragrances, recipes for combining different scents to achieve desired emotional effects will become popular.

The trend toward realism and naturalism will also play out in fashion. We will strive to achieve multi-sensory looks that combine color and style with texture and scent. Cosmetics and personal-care products will satisfy our sensual cravings for indulgences. Fashion designers will experiment with new fiber technologies, even combining new man-made fibers with natural ones that achieve ultra-comfort in our clothes while enhancing feminine curves with fabric that floats and swings, rather than clings. We will look for more washable fabrics, rather than dry cleaning with all those dangerous chemicals. Consumers will have signature fragrances that are individually hand blended to capture the essence of the personality. Personal fragrances will be developed for different moods, allowing the individual to coordinate his or her signature scent with activities for the day or their feelings.

As we ground ourselves more and more in reality, we will want our "techno-toys" to be decidedly Jetson's 21st century. For TVs, home entertainment systems, major appliances, and computers, we will favor an ultra-high-tech look, lots of chrome and steel, lights and buttons, and sleek curves. Our desire for the ultra-high-tech look for technology products will play out in our favorite toy: cars. Today's consumers are enamored of the retro-looking Chrysler PT Cruiser, Ford Thunderbird, and the new GM Chevy Bel Air Concept Vehicle, but car design will take a decidedly high-tech turn soon. It will offer designs that look forward by looking back to the future vision of motor-vehicle transportation, as conceived in the 1940s and 1950s.

CONSUMER TREND | Time is the new shopping currency

If the rising economy of the 1990s taught us anything, it was that anyone who is willing to get the right education and work hard at the right job can make more money. However, we also discovered that no matter how rich or poor we were, no one could add one second more to one's life. Time is the great social equalizer. We all have only 24 hours a day, 7 days a week, 365 days per year. With this discovery comes the awareness that our time is a precious and limited resource. A new priority of making the most of the limited time we have is taking over. Consumers are looking at all the ways they spend their time, including shopping, and demanding a more time-efficient, time-conscious way to shop.

The amount of time consumers are willing to shop has declined steadily over the past decade, and it can be expected to collapse even more as consumers are confronted with new concerns about safety in public places. America's Research Group found that consumers who visited 2 to 3 stores in 1990 to buy home furnishings, electronics, and major appliances, had cut the number of visits back by 0.5 stores by the end of the decade. Today, shoppers are going to only 1.8 stores to make the same purchases.

Further, as consumers retreat into the safety and comfort of their homes, they want to spend less time at the store, especially a store that is not satisfying their craving for a unique and emotionally satisfying experience. They will do more of their weekly shopping in a single shopping trip, so they can get back home and to safety more quickly. More consumer shopping will also be done from the home, with consumers turning to the internet, mail-order catalogs, even party-based and other direct-selling businesses, for their shopping needs.

Party plans and other forms of direct selling will be the next guerilla marketing method to grab share, while giving fits to traditional retailers in the years to come. This retailing methodology has everything going for it in today's emotional climate. You get a chance to meet and greet your friends in the safety of a friend's home, thus providing social experiences that people desire. Over appetizers and a glass of wine, you get to look at new, interesting products presented by your friend, a spokesperson you can really trust. While seeing the new products, you can learn how to use them or display them in innovative ways, thus providing the enhancement of education and information. You gain access to special sales offers, and you can pay for the products later when they are delivered to your home. It is the perfect retailing method for the new millennium. Longaberger Baskets, Blyth's PartyLite candles, Pampered Chef, Discovery Toys, Avon, Mary Kay, and many others have known it for years, and soon many other smart marketers will be exploring opportunities to sell in this way. *Word of warning*: It only works with women, at least so far.

Television shopping mimics the intimacy of party plans. We are already conditioned to think of the television celebrities we invite into our homes everyday as our "friends." As a result, the television shopping channels with their personally engaging show hosts will become a more powerful retailing media in the future.

CONSUMER TREND | Coming retail crisis: excess retail space

It is happening in office space today. Office real estate is facing a crisis of excess inventory. After years of building new office space coupled with overly optimistic tenants who grabbed more office space than they needed, nearly 40 million square feet of office space will return to the market in 2002, according to Torto Wheaton Research. As new office buildings remain vacant and existing tenants fail to renew their leases, rents will fall and overall office vacancy rates will rise. Even boom towns like Atlanta, Dallas, and Houston face office vacancy rates in the double-digits as we enter 2002.

As a crisis grows in office real estate, so too will one develop in commercial retail space. The results of over-building retail space in the 1990s will come home to roost soon. Today every man, woman, and child "owns" between 40 and 50 square feet of dedicated retail space. In the 1990s, about 3 square feet per person was added to total retail space inventory. With 44,500 shopping centers nationwide, 300 million square feet of new store space was added in 2000. During the 1990s, space devoted to retail grew 20 percent, twice as fast as the population. Consequently, operating profits for retailers have dropped, and the retail business has become far more competitive.

Contributing to the coming retail crisis is the shifting pattern of consumer shopping. Consumers are turning away from traditional department stores and shopping more at mass merchants, discounters, and warehouse marts. While the sales from general merchandisers in total rose 64 percent from 1992 to 2000, the key driver of growth in this segment was the category of other general retailers, including Wal-Mart, Kmart, Target, Costco, and Sam's Club. Posting growth of 141 percent from 1992 to 2000, the other general retailers comprised of discounters and warehouse clubs reached $170.9 billion in retail revenue. In the same eight-year period, traditional department stores sales grew only 34 percent, not even matching growth of the retail industry as a whole. Non-store retailers also posted triple-digit growth from 1992 to 2000. Non-store retailers include catalogers and mail-order marketers, television shopping, direct sales, party-plan marketers, and e-tailers. This segment rose 121 percent from $73.4 billion in sales in 1992 to $162 billion in 2000. Growth of these two segments—other general merchandisers and non-store retailers—is expected to outpace that of the retail industry as a whole. These two segments will continue to grab market share by siphoning sales away from competing classes of retailers.

A bright spot in the retail marketplace has been the explosive growth of large, national, specialty chains, including Bed Bath & Beyond, Linens 'n Things, Pier 1, Pottery Barn, Williams-Sonoma, Restoration Hardware, Home Depot, Lowe's, and so forth. These national, specialty retailers are literally "eating the lunch" of small independent specialty retailers that specialize in gift and home products. Yet, the national specialty chains have an Achilles' heel that may soon start to trip them up. Many of these companies have become retail "darlings" by posting consistent annual growth rates in the range of 7 to 15 percent. However, that growth has come from opening new stores rather than increases in existing-store sales. The trouble is that with only about 225 U.S. cities boasting a total population of 100,000

RETAIL SALES BY TYPE OF STORE, 1992 AND 2000

in $ billions, excludes motor vehicles, gasoline, and food service

	1992	2000	change 1992-2000
Furnishings and electronics	$97.8	$179.3	83%
Building and garden	160.2	277.2	73
Food and beverage	371.5	465.3	25
Health and personal care	90.8	158.4	74
Clothing and accessories	120.3	168.5	40
Sporting goods and hobby/books	49.3	79.6	61
General merchandise total	248.0	407.8	64
Department store	177.1	236.9	34
Other general	70.8	170.9	141
Miscellaneous stores	55.8	108.6	95
Non-store	73.4	162.2	121
Total retail trade	**1267.0**	**2006.9**	**58**

Source: Bureau of Economic Analysis, U.S. Census Bureau
Note: Numbers may not add to totals due to rounding.

or more, the new markets where the national, specialty retailers can open is shrinking. Many of the chains have between 200 and 300 individual stores, and behemoth Pier 1 has just topped 900 outlets. Inevitably, revenue growth for these chains will return to earth as their "frontier" markets evaporate. Their new store openings will be slated for existing markets where they will start to cannibalize their own stores' sales.

The coming retail shakeout will have an impact on all retailers, large and small. Clearly, some big-name department stores will be unable to stay the course as the department-store sector continues to distance itself from the shopping needs of consumers. More small independent retailers, those shops that line small-town-America's main streets, will fold as Wal-Mart, Kmart, or Target open up on the town's bypass. The national, specialty chains will have to work harder for every percentage point of revenue growth, as their building expansion programs slow. They may well start to close some of the unproductive stores in favor of larger stores in growing urban or suburban centers. Many older malls will fold as consumers start to patronize the new, unenclosed, lifestyle malls that are sprouting up throughout the country. They are designed to mimic small-town ambiance, while showcasing national, upscale, and specialty, chain stores.

WHAT CAN RETAILERS DO TO SURVIVE THE COMING SHAKEOUT?

The lessons of this book—understanding why people buy—apply equally to manufacturers and retail businesses in anticipating consumer behavior now and in the future. Retailers need to explore with their shoppers why people shop in their stores. What features, products, attributes, benefits, needs, and consumer desires does the store meet? In what areas does it fail to satisfy? Retailers need to dig deeper than simply "customer service" and "quality." Too many retailers imagine their point of difference is "customer service" or "quality" products, but if you sit in a room for five minutes with consumers, you discover that these terms are meaningless. Retailers have to understand the heart, mind, and emotions of their customers. They need to figure out what experiences consumers expect and desire to have while shopping in the store and then develop strategies to give them more of those experiences.

Customer service has to be more than answering a question, wrapping a package, or escorting the customer to an aisle. Retail salespeople need to participate in the shopping experience with their customers. They have to be shopping partners, not salespeople or clerks. They have to have authentic enthusiasm. They need to be real and honest. They need to be likeable. They need to like their customers.

Retailers can also enhance the shopping experience by providing information. Why should Home Depot have a monopoly on teaching people how to use their products? Any retailer selling home products can figure out hundreds of ways to provide information to its customers. Just watch HGTV, The Learning Channel, or Discovery to figure out how. The same theory applies to retailers of electronics, books, pet supplies, cosmetics and personal care, gourmet foods, housewares, sporting goods, hobby items, and crafts supplies. Consumers are eager to learn about their passion and willing to participate with retailers in this process. The key to launching a successful experiential-retailing program is to provide valuable information without substituting a sales presentation for a learning experience. Consumers are too savvy today. They will immediately see through the hoax.

Finally, the retail mantra "location-location-location" will never fade. Retailers need to be where shoppers shop. When shoppers stop coming to your street, your strip center, your mall, you'd better move and fast. Today's shoppers are more time sensitive; they are not going to go out of their way and use up valuable time driving to this store and that one. They are going to look for the easiest, most time-effective way to complete their shopping. Retailers need to be where the shoppers are. We are already seeing the future of the shift in consumer shopping patterns. Retailers need to anticipate the shopping shifts in their local markets and be ready to move before it is too late.

Chapter 7

PULLING IT ALL TOGETHER HOW TO SELL MORE

Now that we have explored the many facets of why people buy things they don't need and learned how the "why" drives and directs consumer behavior, we have a final task. We need to look at the strategies that evolve from this investigation. We need to learn how to get people to buy more of the things they don't need. Marketing guru Sergio Zyman says the chief aim of marketing is to sell more things, to more people, more often for more money. We need to learn how to harness the power of "why" in our marketing and brand-building strategies.

Marketers that use "why people buy" strategies in their marketing go beyond the purely tactical realm (i.e., price, distribution, advertising, media placement, and so forth) and into a future-oriented, long term view of the business, the brand, and the marketplace. This future-oriented, strategic realm is where loyal consumer relationships form.

Today's marketing watchwords, "emotional branding" and "emotion marketing," are beginning to scratch the surface of a "why people buy" strategy. With their recognition of the emotional side of marketing and branding, marketers are becoming aware that consumer behavior is not based solely upon reason and logic, but driven by the heart and the emotions. Yet the emotional realm is complex, highly individualized and very personal; it takes a unique approach to get inside of the hearts of the consumer. Left-brain-dominated marketing executives employing left-brain-oriented research strategies to develop left-brain marketing tactics are destined to falter as they are confounded by the emotions of their marketplace. By ignoring "why people buy" in favor of focusing on who, what, where, when, how, and how much of consumer behavior, the left-brain-oriented marketing companies are forever going to be chasing their market.

"Why people buy"-informed marketing strategies must be supported by strong left-brain-oriented tactics and approaches, but marketing executives informed with "why people buy" insights will be able to anticipate the shifts and turns in their market. They will move just ahead of their customers, knowing where they are going to be next, and what the customers will demand when they get there. Do not misunderstand the strategy. Future marketing success is based on marrying the two points of view, the qualitative and the quantitative, the intuitive and the rational, the right brain and the left brain, the why people buy, and the who, what, where, how, and how much.

Here are the basic strategies in "why people buy:"

Touch the emotions of your customers

Consumers make decisions to purchase discretionary products largely based upon emotion because there is no strictly rational reason for buying something you don't need. However, even in the purchase of necessary products, consumer's emotions are engaged. After hundreds of hours spent talking to and interacting with consumers in a research setting, I know that emotion is at the foundation of people buying things they don't need. Reason is always secondary in the purchase decision.

A word of caution to marketers: If you do not think this is true, then you have been listening to the words consumers say, not the *way* they say them. In focus groups, I have seen men, in particular, trying to act so rational in explaining their purchasing behavior, yet when they are given an exercise designed to reveal the underlying emotions, their eyes light up and they get excited. In these settings, I have seen grown men turn into little boys before me. Their emotions take over, and that is where they ultimately make their purchase decisions. I even think that these men have convinced themselves they act rationally, but they prove the deception on camera in the focus group.

Because consumers make purchase decisions in the emotional realm, they are highly responsive to environmental cues and clues that stimulate and communicate on an emotional level. Marketers need to make sure that the emotional messages they send are in keeping with the emotional needs of the customers. Design of products, packaging, advertising, and logos resonate on an emotional level. Color sends strong emotional clues, so marketers need to use color effectively in packaging, as well as in the color palette of the product.

Involving shoppers with the product or the ad establishes a connection. Most companies pay too little attention to heightening consumer involvement through in-store and point-of-purchase displays. Brand and product awareness are no longer the endgame. You need to get consumers to do something with your product—pick it up, touch it, or interact in a multi-sensory way. That is what will imprint the brand in the shopper's consciousness and begin to establish an emotional connection with the customer.

Give customers rational justifiers so they will have permission to buy

Emotions may lead, but justifiers close the deal in the subtle commercial seduction between a product and a consumer. Some products need few justifiers to get the consumer to buy. Products that give immediate emotional gratification and do not require the consumer to make any kind of sacrifice are indulgences that demand few justifiers. On the other hand, a purchase that is more costly, more utilitarian, or more luxurious and extravagant, requires elaborate justifiers to encourage the consumer to complete the sale. Marketers need to do the hard work of creating the justifiers for the customer. Far more than just presenting product benefits and features, marketers need to understand *why people buy,* to provide meaningful, wide-ranging justifiers that support consumers in their purchase decisions.

As discussed in Chapter Four, our research reveals that improving the quality of life is the top justifier that consumers use and the one that truly resonates at an emotional level with most of them. Marketers need to explore deeply and completely how their products improve the quality of their customers' lives, then make sure all marketing communications—advertising, packaging, and point-of-purchase—communicate the quality-of-life-enhancing values back to them.

Appeal to customers who are in motion

A closely guarded secret that direct marketers have known for years is that the most recent purchasers and the most frequent purchasers are the best prospects for buying again. Like eating potato chips, shoppers rarely stop after buying just one thing. One purchase leads to another and another, often with the first purchase justifying a continued spending spree. The emotionally driven consumer often behaves gluttonously, seeking more consuming satisfaction from buying more things.

Every shopper who wanders into a store, stands before a display window, reads an advertisement, or watches an ad is a prospect. They must be romanced into buying something, to come into the store, or to seek out more information about the store or the product advertised. Romance is not played out rationally like a chess game; it is conducted emotionally. Moreover, I will share another secret: consumers want desperately to be romanced when they shop. It makes them feel special, unique, valuable, valued. Ultimately, the only way to truly romance customers is to love them. It may sound hokey as we talk in the context of the commercial relationship of a company and its customer, but everyone wants to be loved. If you really care about your customers, want the best for them, want happiness and satisfaction for them, then you will find the right strategy. I have seen companies that disrespect their customers, do not value them, and do not understand that everything, ultimately, starts with the customer. Every company owes its being to the customer, and employees are dependent upon customers for their weekly paychecks. However, some companies do not make that understanding part of their corporate values. How many of us, as customers, have faced surly employees and store clerks who act as if we are in their way? These companies cannot succeed because their interaction with their customers is based on deception.

> **Every company owes its being to the customer.**

Marketers need to respond to consumers in motion to sell more. They have to think about ways to cross merchandise products creatively to open new consuming opportunities. Like the retailing of major appliances we looked at in Chapter One, marketers need to think from the point of view of customers: what *they* want, what *they* need, where *they* might want to find it. Companies need to stop making decisions based upon their own myopic point of view—what the company wants to sell, where it wants to sell it, and how it wants to sell it. Tactical business decisions made from the point of view of what is best for the company, its operations, and its employees will fail. Companies must adapt their operations to the consumer, not the other way around. Truly put the customer first, and watch how your sales skyrocket.

Make customers feel like winners every time

Customers shop to satisfy emotional needs and longings, and they want their shopping experience to provide emotional satisfaction as well. When they shop, they want to feel like winners, as if they did something good, fun, and beneficial for themselves and their families, including saving money. It is more than just finding a great bargain, but when shoppers do find a super deal, it makes them feel like winners. When consumers feel they have done something outstanding, found something extraordinary, achieved some great height, become unique, more special, more lovable, better, they feel like winners. When customers leave the store with your company's products in their shopping bags, you want them to be happy and satisfied. It is so much more than price, but few marketers go the extra step to discover new, creative ways to make customers feel like winners.

Making customers feel like winners goes back to our earlier strategy of helping them enhance the quality of their lives. Make their lives special, more meaningful, more satisfying, more fulfilling. Things do not buy happiness, but things can enhance the life experience that leads to happiness. Consumers feel like winners when they can trade money, such a mundane thing, for the experience of greater happiness, fulfillment, and satisfaction.

Help your customers fulfill their fantasies

Advertising agencies have created consuming fantasies for years. They carefully select models, images, settings, scenes, and story lines to evoke an image, a feeling, and a fantasy of how one's life would be transformed through owning a product. I want to live in the world of laundry detergent commercials. In those ads, the day is always sunny and the trees are always green. There is beautiful music playing in the background and the curtains are gently swaying in a mild breeze. It is never too cold or hot in laundry-detergent world and it always smells fresh and clean. Perhaps the craft of advertising taught consumers how to create consuming fantasies, but however it started, consumers invent often elaborate fantasies that they desire to act out through the things they buy and own.

When consumers talk about why they buy, they often explain it in terms of fantasy fulfillment. Through their consuming fantasies, they imagine how they will enhance their lives by the purchase of some thing, and how it will taste, feel, smell, look, and sound. They are vis-

ceral in their fantasies and use them to build excitement and anticipation leading toward a purchase. Marketers must tap into those consuming fantasies, understand them, and play back the fantasy imagery
in marketing communications. It is part of romancing customers, relat-
ing on an emotional level, and making them feel special and loved.

Entertain, entertain, entertain

Consumers crave entertainment as a means to escape their mundane,
ordinary, humdrum lives. Entertainment offers a respite from melan-
choly and feelings of hopelessness. Being entertained is more than
just watching a movie or a television show; it is about
engaging the mind in a fantasy that offers escape from the
boring facets of daily life. Entertainment is about reaching
out and linking with other people, other realities, and
another consciousness. It is pondering a painting, walking
in the woods, climbing a mountain, attending a party,
going to the mall, walking the streets of New York, or vis-
iting an historic home. Our longing for experiences is all about being
entertained.

The "why" is the contract with the consumer.

An educated mind is an active mind, and an active mind needs
mental stimulation. Marketers and retailers in the future need to plan
to satisfy this need. It is a great opportunity just waiting for them. It
will build lasting relationships with consumers and keep them coming back for more.

Translate the brand into the "why"

In a recent discussion with a client about why people buy his company's product and the implications for the brand, he had a "eureka"
moment. He became animated and blurted out, "The 'why' is the
brand!" All I could say was "exactly," as he so succinctly and elo-
quently expressed what I had been saying.

The promise, implicit in the relationship between the brand and the
consumer is "why people buy." The promise includes the fantasies
they have about the brand, the wishes they want fulfilled, and the way
the brand enhances their quality of life. The brand must satisfy the
promise, and if you as a brand manager and marketer do not really
understand the promise encompassed in "why people buy," then you
are destined to fall short of their desires. The "why" is the contract
with the consumer, the agreement that binds the brand with the con-

sumer. If you do not intimately understand why people buy your brand, then it is only hit or miss that the brand will connect with the consumer.

In all the research and planning that the Coca-Cola Company did in developing "New Coke," it apparently never researched "why people buy" Coke. Rather, it assumed it had something to do with consumers' thirst and their taste preferences. It conducted tactical research about what combinations of flavors were in tune with consumers because Coca-Cola executives thought that people bought Coke because of the taste. They learned that even when they got the taste formula aligned with consumers' preferences in blind taste tests, they got it dead wrong as a brand. People drink Coke because it links them with happy memories of their childhood and recalls the lovely fantasies Coke commercials have spawned over the years. Consumers have a deep love of the brand and buy what the brand promises and the fantasies it fulfills, not just flavored soda water. That is the magic of a brand, and the foundation of that magic comes with understanding *why people buy.*

GAIN BIG VISION BY FOCUSING ON WHY PEOPLE BUY

In my work as a marketing consultant, I run into two types of clients: little-vision companies and big-vision companies. Little-vision companies want market research and advice that is tactically oriented. They have immediate marketing problems and need information to help them make tactical decisions, related to product, pricing, advertising, distribution, and sales. Their focus is on next quarter, or the next six months, or next year. While they are caught in the day-to-day struggles of running a business, they will achieve only incremental improvements taking a little-vision approach. There is nothing wrong with incremental improvements. Every company can use incremental gains, but the marketing problems and challenges faced today are insignificant when compared with the challenges companies will confront in the future, especially if they maintain a little-vision approach to marketing. Ultimately, little-vision companies end up chasing their customers, trying desperately to keep up with them as they change, shift, and evolve.

Big-vision companies, on the other hand, are looking two, three, or five years out. They understand that tactics follow strategy. They know they have to have a strategic vision so they can create their future. Big-vision companies are not stuck on tactics or paralyzed by uncertainties. Their foresight yields exponential growth. By understanding *why people buy*, they can anticipate the shifts and bends in the consumer market. Hockey player Wayne Gretzky, when asked what made him play better than anyone else, responded that the other players skated to where the puck was, but that he skated to where the puck was going. This is a metaphor of how big-vision companies operate. They anticipate where their customers are going to be in the future and are waiting for consumers when they get there.

Only big-vision companies can successfully implement brand building and strategy. Little-vision companies define their brands too narrowly and too specifically for the here and now. In comparison, big-vision companies take a long-term view of the brand and its customers. Therefore, they create a brand strategy that is encompassing, timeless, and emotionally compelling. Big-vision companies understand that "why people buy" remains stable over time, and it is the secret to understanding consumer behavior today as well as how it will change in the future. Little-vision companies ignore completely the *why*, but instead focus only on consumer behavior—who, what, where, how, when, how much. Consequently, they will forever be second guessing consumers and trying to catch up to them.

Gap Inc. exemplifies how a company can go awry when it fails to infuse its marketing and branding programs with "why people buy" strategy. Gap Inc. was doing great as an apparel retailer selling basic, high-quality casual clothes with youthful zing at a good value to a wide-ranging consumer market. It faltered when it launched the Old Navy brand. Old Navy had the same basic "why people buy" values as the Gap brand did. Old Navy was everything that Gap was, only cheaper. Old Navy and Gap became synonymous from the consumers' perspective, with Old Navy's less expensive positioning and perceived lower product quality dragging down the more high-quality, value-oriented price positioning of Gap. The company perceived that it created a point of difference by keeping Gap stores in malls and making Old Navy stores freestanding. But that was wrong! Consumers don't care where the stores are located. They just want to buy products when they think about them. Gap Inc. has got to do some serious work to extricate its core Gap brand from Old Navy and establish each brand uniquely based upon "why people buy" strategy.

For too long, marketing executives have focused almost exclusively on studying consumer behavior. However, they have been using left-brained tools that track the past and provide only tactical direction. While marketers know they need to get out in front of their market-place and anticipate the changes that are occurring there, they do not know how to do it. It really is quite straightforward. You just have to ask the right question and be open to the implications when your customers answer you. That question is simple, "Why do people buy?"

Big Vision	**Little Vision**
Strategic	Tactical
Long range, next two years, five years, ten years	Short term, next quarter, next year
Why People Buy	What, where, how, when, how much
Exponential Growth	Incremental improvements
Future Vision	Rear-view mirror
Anticipate the market	Chase the market

My wish for you, and the reason I wrote this book, is that you incorporate the "why people buy" approach, thinking, and strategy into your marketing plans.

Bibliography

Bourdieu, Pierre, translated by Richard Nice. *Distinction: A Social Critique of the Judgement of Taste*. Cambridge, MA: Harvard University Press, 1984.

Catalano, Ellen Mohn and Nina Sonenberg. *Consuming Passions:Help for Compulsive Shoppers*. Oakland, CA: New Harbinger Publications, 1993.

Clapp, Rodney, editor. *The Consuming Passion: Christianity & the Consumer Culture*. Downers Grove, IL: InterVarsity Press, 1998.

DeGraaf, John, David Wann and Thmas H. Naylor. *Affluenza: The All-Consuming Epidemic*. San Francisco: Berrett-Koehler Publishers, Inc., 2001.

Frank, Robert H. *Luxury Fever: Money and Happiness in an Era of Excess*. Princeton, NJ: Princeton University Press, 1999.

Popcorn, Faith and Lys Marigold. *EVEolution: The Eight Truths of Marketing to Women*. New York: Hyperion, 2000.

Rosenblatt, Roger, editor. *Consuming Desires: Consumption, Culture, and the Pursuit of Happiness*. Washington, DC: Island Press, 1999.

Schorr, Juliet B. *The Overspent American: Why We Want What We Don't Need*. New York: HarperPerennial, 1998.

Schorr, Juliet B. forward by Ralph Nader. *Do Americans Shop too Much?* Boston, MA: Beacon Press, 2000

Schulz, Eric. *The Marketing Game: How the World's Best Companies*

Play to Win. Holbrook, MA: Adams Media Corporation, 2001.

Twitchell, James B. *Lead Us Into Temptation: The Triumph of American Materialism.* New York: Columbia University Press, 1999.

Underhill, Paco. *Why We Buy: The Science of Shopping.* New York: Simon & Schuster, 1999.

Veblen, Thorstein. *The Theory of the Leisure Class.* New York: Penguin Books, 1899.

Zyman, Sergio. *The End of Marketing as We Know It.* New York: Harper Business, 2000.

INDEX

ABOUT THE AUTHOR

Pam Danziger is the founder and president of Unity Marketing, a marketing consulting firm serving consumer-product businesses selling luxury and discretionary products. Her work is designed to help companies capture more market share and build brand equity by deepening their understanding of their customers.

Ms. Danziger is a nationally recognized expert in consumer marketing and psychology. She has appeared on NBC's *Today Show*, CBS News *Sunday Morning*, Fox News, and NPR's *Marketplace*. She has been quoted by, among others, *The Wall Street Journal, The New York Times, American Demographics, Forbes, USA Today, Associated Press, Los Angeles Times,* and *The Chicago Tribune*. In addition, she speaks frequently at industry trade shows and professional conferences.

With a B.A. degree in English Literature from Pennsylvania State University and a Master of Library Science degree from the University of Maryland, Pam long ago traded in the Dewey Decimal card catalog for computerized databases. She has been surveying, analyzing, classifying, and researching information to solve business problems ever since. Before founding Unity Marketing in 1992, Pam worked for a major Washington trade association and Bell Communications Research. Her last job was at Franklin Mint where she was director of competitive analysis, gathering marketing information to identify trends in the collectibles market.

Pam is currently at work on her next book, *Reinventing Luxury: The Power to Pursue your Passions.*

Pam Danziger
Unity Marketing
717-336-1600; 717-336-1601 FAX
www.unitymarketingonline.com